Sports Illustrated™

KOBE BRYANT

A TRIBUTE TO A BASKETBALL LEGEND

CONTENTS

"People say I've made it, but I haven't come close to being where I want to be."
—Kobe Bryant

KOBE BRYANT

LAKERS
24
LAKERS
24

Bryant holds the ball in front of the Lakers faithful at Staples Center in 2008.

THE PHENOM

Bryant floats through the lane against the Jazz at the Forum in 1998.

Chapter 1

Excerpted from SPORTS ILLUSTRATED, May 6, 1996

School's Out

Philadelphia schoolboy Kobe Bryant is headed straight for the NBA

BY MICHAEL BAMBERGER

On Monday at 2:25 p.m., the final bell rang at Lower Merion High, in the leafy suburbs of Philadelphia, and the school's gymnasium, a museum piece circa 1964, began to fill. Boys with knapsacks on their backs scurried up the bleachers, and girls with lacrosse sticks in their hands sat cross-legged on the hardwood floor. Teachers, feigning disinterest, filled the gym's double doors.

The school's athletic director, wearing his best suit and tie, tested the microphone.

On the edge of the basketball floor reporters from *The Main Line Times* and from the *Merionite*, the school newspaper, accustomed to covering events at the creaking gym without competition, found themselves making space for ESPN and *The Washington Post*. Members of Boyz II Men, who hail from Philadelphia and are friends of the featured speaker, hovered in the back. The name of the singing group never seemed more appropriate. On Monday at 2:35 p.m., in the same gym where he scored more schoolboy basketball points than anybody will remember, an amiable prodigy named Kobe Bryant, 17 years old, announced his plans for the future. He couldn't, after all, be a Lower Merion Ace forever. But what would come next? La Salle University, where his father, Joe (Jellybean) Bryant, is an assistant basketball coach? Villanova? Michigan? The NBA, where Joe spent eight seasons with the San Diego Clippers, the Philadelphia 76ers, and the Houston Rockets?

Bryant, a 6'6" shuffler—except on a basketball court, where he moves like lightning—ambled up to the podium in a ventless sport coat and fine dress trousers bought at the last minute and in need of a tailor, his sunglasses positioned on the top of his shiny shaved head. His coat had puffy shoulders, masking his frame, which at 190 pounds is as skinny and malleable as a strand of cooked spaghetti. He leaned his goofy kid's mouth toward the microphone, mockingly

Bryant spent 16 days as a Charlotte Hornet before his rights were traded to the Lakers in July 1996.

Lakers GM Jerry West (left) and coach Del Harris introduce Kobe Bryant to the press.

brought his fingers to his unblemished chin as if he were still pondering his decision, and delivered the news that insiders had been expecting for a week.

"I've decided to skip college and take my talent to the NBA," Bryant said.

The gymnasium at Lower Merion, a school of high academic achievement, filled with whooping. Bryant—a B student who scored 1,080 on his SATs and speaks fluent Italian, which he learned while living in Italy during the half-dozen years his father played professional basketball there—was beaming.

He will enter the NBA draft on June 26 and will be, league scouts and general managers say, one of the first 13 players chosen, a lottery pick. In his first four years in the NBA, if he plays four years in the NBA, Bryant could earn $10 million—or more. Of course, he could also spend those four years earning a college degree. He chose to pass up that option, he said, not because of money or parental pressure or a desire to emulate Kevin Garnett, the teenage forward for the Minnesota Timberwolves who went from Farragut Academy in Chicago to the No. 5 pick in last year's NBA draft and proved by midseason that he belonged in the league. Bryant's family does not need the money, and his parents did not influence his decision. He's going pro to fulfill a dream.

"Playing in the NBA has been my dream since I was three," Bryant said, and he's old enough to know that a dream deferred can peter out to nothingness. He is taking no chances, not after averaging 31 points, 12 rebounds, seven assists, four blocks, and four steals a game in leading the Aces to the state class AAAA title as a senior.

What, precisely, he will do in the NBA is anybody's guess. In the last three decades only six U.S. players have joined the NBA without playing college basketball, and all of them have been big men, centers and power forwards: Moses Malone, Darryl Dawkins, Bill Willoughby, Shawn Kemp, Thomas Hamilton, and Garnett. Bryant played the entire floor in high school—his Lower Merion coach, Gregg Downer, compared Bryant's style of play with Michael Jordan's and Grant Hill's—and could score seemingly at will from inside. The cumulative effect of all those inside points was to give him a reputation as the best high school basketball player in the country.

In the pros he will be a guard, but whether he's an NBA shooter remains to be determined. Also unclear is whether a 17-year-old who is truly happy with a book in his hands should be going straight into the workforce without stopping for a college education.

"I think it's a total mistake," says the Boston Celtics' director of basketball development, Jon Jennings, who opposes any schoolboy's going pro. "Kevin Garnett was the best high school player I ever saw, and I wouldn't have advised him to jump to the NBA. And Kobe is no Kevin Garnett."

That note was not sounded at the Lower Merion gym on Monday. The athletic director, Tom McGovern, set the tone. "In the last four years he's brought us joy, happiness, national recognition—and a state title," McGovern said. "We will be behind him 100 percent. We owe him that much."

Bryant won the NBA Slam Dunk Contest in 1997, becoming the youngest player ever to claim the trophy.

MALONE
32

Bryant glides past Utah's Karl Malone in the playoffs in 1997.

8

Bryant never shrank from comparisons to Michael Jordan.

Lakers legend Magic Johnson on the sideline with Bryant at the All-Star Game in Madison Square Garden in 1998.

Excerpted from SPORTS ILLUSTRATED, April 27, 1998

Show Time!

Is Kobe Bryant the second coming of Magic or Michael? The playoffs are the place to find out if he's truly a prodigy or merely a creature of hype

BY IAN THOMSEN

Last December, before the Los Angeles Lakers' annual pilgrimage to Chicago, the team's director of public relations, John Black, quietly warned 19-year-old Kobe Bryant that the press was about to open public hearings into the matter of whether he was, indeed, the next Michael Jordan. Bryant could have gone into a slump right then.

"It doesn't bother me," he responded. "I expect to be that good."

Now he was really asking for trouble. For Jordan is the American Zeus, an utterly commercial god who scores, plays defense, wins championships, and appears in the advertisements during timeouts. A few weeks after Bryant had been interviewed for the position in Chicago (he scored 33 points, many of them while being guarded by Jordan, who had 36), he was being promoted on one side of a full-page newspaper ad for the Feb. 8 All-Star Game. On the opposite side of the page was the requisite picture of Jordan, his tongue dangling like a royal flag.

"I said, 'Cool,'" Bryant says. "It was like they were making it out to be some big one-on-one showdown."

Others were more concerned. "Wasn't Harold Miner supposed to have been the next Michael Jordan?" asked New Jersey Nets assistant coach Don Casey. Miner vanished from the league as if he had been caught staring at the Lost Ark of the Covenant. Grant Hill, exhibiting the wisdom of a Duke graduate, seemed to turn away from comparisons with Jordan at the last moment, but the unexplainable forces of the universe punished him nonetheless by making him play for Jordan's former coach, Doug Collins, the screaming Hydra.

It is because Bryant is so completely unaffected by fame that the league and its network partner, NBC, felt they could safely extol his virtues. In so doing, they almost turned him into the anti-Jordan. Western Conference coach

Bryant and Magic Johnson pose for the front cover of the April 27, 1998, issue of Sports Illustrated.

George Karl benched him in the fourth quarter of the All-Star Game, and several of the older players—but then they were all older, weren't they?—were apparently fed up with everything Bryant stood for. Karl Malone recalled trying to set a pick for him. "The guy told me he's got it," the 34-year-old Malone said. "Like I told Coach Karl, when younger guys tell me to get out of the way, that's a game I don't need to be in. I was ticked."

"I still don't remember that play," Bryant says. "I probably did it—I'm sure I did it—but there's nothing wrong with it. I was just being aggressive. When somebody told me what he said, I thought it was funny."

It was not meant to be funny. It was meant to lump Bryant in with the prematurely rewarded nine-figure millionaires of his generation. Malone's complaint is that the league's young stars have walked into a vault of public goodwill and unmarked bills that was unlocked for them by the older players, and they are shortsightedly spending the principal when, really, they should be content just to live off the interest. Their preposterous salaries have given them a sense of power long before many of them have even contended for championships. When Malone, the league's reigning MVP, saw that he had been replaced on the All-Star Game marquee by a 19-year-old who doesn't even start for his club—well, you can't blame Malone for assuming the worst.

Bryant's second NBA season has been one long, inconclusive argument. His play since All-Star weekend has seemed to confirm suspicions that he is a creature of hype. In the 24 games between Feb. 10 and March 25 he shot an anemic 37% from the floor and averaged just 12.1 points, or 5.8 less than he had during the first half of the season. Not the numbers of the next Michael Jordan. Worse, Bryant admits that some of his teammates have confronted him about being selfish on the court. Lakers coach Del Harris has vowed to teach Bryant a lesson about the "team game." Bryant "didn't learn it in high school, and he didn't go to college, so he has to learn it here," says the 60-year-old Harris. "The only way he can learn it is by reduced playing time until he accepts it." During one 10-game stretch after the All-Star break, Harris cut Bryant's playing time by almost seven minutes a game; by the end of the season the chastened Bryant was back near his prebreak average of 26.7 minutes.

But the playoffs are here. The haggling is finished. Over the last month the Lakers have been reinstalling Bryant into their offense with the understanding that they can't go far in the postseason without him. Harris worries, too, that they can't go far with him. The young man is being asked to fulfill his potential immediately. The Lakers need his creativity in the half-court offense, and yet they haven't married themselves to him for better or for worse, in good times and in bad. Will he be the Bryant of the first half of this season, full of energy and confidence, or the Bryant of the second half, who has been fatigued and criticized? The Lakers are going to find out the hard way, by running their engine at the highest temperatures without the proper testing.

Someday, Magic Johnson firmly believes, Bryant is going to look back on this season and realize that he is the only one who remembers his struggles. "People forget," Johnson says, as if speaking about himself.

The believers—Johnson, Jordan, Lakers center Shaquille O'Neal—exhibit the same faith in Bryant that they have in themselves. In him they see a self-made man, a prodigy who taught himself the game by correspondence course. Perhaps no player has ever made more use of his imagination. Compared with the older stars, Bryant seems to have been raised far away in a basketball convent. In truth he was. Where is the incentive to improve if the money and the praise—the full-page advertisements—are lavished on players before they accomplish anything? Johnson looks at many young stars as if they've inherited their wealth; when they actually take over, he worries, the business he helped to build will fall apart. He was especially distressed by the uninspired performances by basketball players at the 1996 Olympics, in which no money changed hands. "A lot of these guys are not worthy and not deserving," he says. "They don't go out and do it for their country. They want the money, but they don't want the responsibility that comes with the money. Kobe is different. He wants all of it."

In Johnson's day TV was just becoming infatuated with the NBA, principally because of him and Larry Bird, and the new exposure made the games seem larger and made the players richer and more famous. That drove the league's profits ever higher, so that a player today can enjoy the life of a champion without winning a title. If Bryant is unique, it might be because he didn't see the game as a way to improve his life. He was connected to the circuit by his father, a former NBA player, and the things Johnson did coursed through the little boy's mind like the blood that pumped through the rest of him. At the same time, Kobe was isolated and sheltered from the excesses of the superstar life. His version of the American Dream differed fundamentally from that of his current NBA peers. They believed in the jackpot. Bryant grew up believing in the mythology.

"My wife and I used to prescreen movies before we'd let the kids see them," says Joe Bryant, Kobe's father. "We used to push the kids under the seat when the actors would start kissing." Joe and his wife, Pam, were still editing Kobe's entertainment a couple of years before he signed his three-year, $3.5 million contract with the Lakers in 1996. He didn't see *The Godfather*, his favorite movie, until last year. "It reminds me of my family," Kobe says. "Not because of the violence, but because of the way they all pulled for each other no matter what."

The Lakers were skeptical when the 17-year-old Bryant came looking for a job a few weeks before the '96 NBA draft. The league's successful high school prodigies—Moses Malone (who began his career in the ABA), Darryl Dawkins, Kevin Garnett—had been big men who were pushed ahead by financial and in some cases academic imperatives. Bryant was different. He was 6'5", which meant that, after playing basketball in the U.S. for less than five years, he was asking teams to wager a first-round pick on his chances of thriving at shooting guard or small forward, arguably the most competitive positions in professional sports. Second, with an SAT score of 1,080, Bryant could have entered most U.S. universities on his academic talents alone, and third, his family didn't need the money; his father had recently completed a 16-year playing career in the NBA and Europe.

When Lakers general manager Jerry West asked Bryant to jump, he might have thought he was watching a coiled spring release: Bryant touched the top of the backboard square. West then put him through a kind of obstacle course, pitting him against Michael Cooper, the former Lakers defensive whiz who used to guard Bird. Cooper bullied and shoved Bryant, trying to use his strength and experience, but the youth moved like a fish under water. West then introduced Bryant to Dontae' Jones, the star of Mississippi State's 1996 Final Four team who was also working out for the Lakers and would be drafted in the first round by the New York Knicks. Both young men were starving for opportunity. A ball was tossed between them, and everyone stood back. Bryant devoured the moment smoothly, like a lion with excellent table manners.

West turned to an aide and said with a buried giggle, "I've seen enough. Let's go." West, who calls Bryant the best prospect he has ever put through a workout, was so impressed that he arranged to send the Lakers' starting center, Vlade Divac, to the Charlotte Hornets for Bryant, whom the Hornets chose with the 13th pick. Freed of Divac's salary, the Lakers

Not quite yet a household name, Bryant was present for Media Day in 1999.

then signed O'Neal to a seven-year, $120 million contract, restoring the team to title contention for the first time since Johnson's better days.

The Lakers still aren't sure how Bryant made up so much ground so fast. "Kobe is at least as mature as any player we have now," West says, "and you cannot discount his family's contribution to that."

But how did a teenager learn the fundamentals so thoroughly while spending the better part of eight years in relative basketball isolation in Europe? The smartest general manager in the game has no ready explanation. He finds himself saying, "You watch Stevie Wonder and you marvel at how he and Ray Charles have overcome handicaps, yet they are wonderfully talented and gifted."

When Joe Bryant left La Salle in 1975 after his junior year to turn professional, it was because his family needed the money. "The rule back then was that you had to prove that you were in financial hardship," he says. He was a 6'9" forward with a guard's mentality, and he was chosen in the first round by the Golden State Warriors. He held out for more money. The Philadelphia 76ers traded for him, offering a reported $900,000 over five years, and that, he says, was that. "I was on the East Coast, so they put me under the basket," he says. "That used to be big, that East Coast-West Coast argument: If Magic had been in New York, would he have had the same kind of freedom he had in L.A.?"

Kobe was born a year after the 1977 NBA Finals, the premature peak of his father's eight-year NBA career. (Joe was a defensive specialist on the Sixers' second unit, behind Julius Erving and George McGinnis, as Philadelphia was dissected in six games by Bill Walton's Portland Trail Blazers.) Kobe, Joe says, "was named after a Kobe steak house in King of Prussia, Pennsylvania. But I don't know if I should say that, because they might want the rights to his name."

In 1984, after Joe had finished his NBA career with the Houston Rockets, he and Pam and their three children set off on a family adventure with all kinds of unforeseen benefits. They moved to Rieti, Italy, where Joe began his European playing career. For eight years, during which he played for four teams, he moved his family from one town to the next like an actor in the theater, settling wherever he could find a production that had a role for him. In the meantime his son was developing a romance with basketball that he might never have experienced in America.

Six-year-old Kobe was enrolled in first grade in a school in Rieti where his two sisters—Shaya, then seven, and Sharia, eight—were entering the second and third grades, respectively. Because they were just learning to speak Italian, they had to work harder than other students. Perhaps had Kobe been a star soccer player, he would have been treated as someone sacred, but his talent for basketball carried no great weight. "In Italy they told me, 'You're a great player over here, but when you get over to America, it won't be like that,'" he recalls.

Basketball became his private hobby, and he had little choice but to be humble about it. "After school I would be the only guy on the basketball court, working on my moves, and then kids would start showing up with their soccer ball," he says. "I could hold them off if there were two or three of them, but when they got to be 11 or 12, I had to give up the court. It was either go home or be the goalkeeper."

By U.S. standards Kobe and his sisters enjoyed an unusually well-rounded life: The streets were safe at all hours, and children mixed easily with their parents in the bright cafe bars. "In America, families break apart because the son has to take a job in South Dakota," Joe Bryant says. "In Italy you'd see whole families living in one big villa. That's what our kids saw. We would go have a meal and end up sitting at the table, eating and talking, for three or four hours."

The Italians were impassioned believers in their basketball clubs, carrying team flags and scarves and wearing their team colors. Fans would throw coins at visiting players, hop in place together, chant in a single voice or sing in a bellow throughout each game. Whether Joe was playing for Reggio di Calabria near Sicily or Pistoia to the north—the sorts of small towns where Italian basketball thrives—he was a cult figure, a 30-points-per-game scorer, the direct opposite of his role in the NBA. "They used to sing songs for my father," Kobe says, and in Italian he sings one: "You know the player who's better than Magic or Jabbar? It's Joseph, Joseph Bryant!"

"If we upset one of the big teams in Italy, I didn't have to pay for a meal for the rest of the week," Joe recalls, laughing. "One year we upset somebody, and the town was like a festival. So much passion."

During the week Joe would practice with his club twice a day, a time-wasting European custom, but for the first time in his working life he took his meals at home. His club would play every Sunday and occasionally in midweek. On Saturday afternoons he would take the family for walks into the mountains. On Monday, his usual day off, Americans who were playing for other Italian clubs would bring their families and meet in the nearest big city—Florence, Rome, Venice—at McDonald's. Sharia and Shaya remember making friends with the daughters of ex-Sixer Harvey Catchings, Tauja and Tamika, who are now basketball stars at Illinois and Tennessee, respectively. "I have pictures of them walking through Venice with Kobe," Joe Bryant says.

On weekdays after school Joe would take Kobe to practice with him, something he couldn't have done in the NBA. While the team worked out, Kobe would shoot baskets in a corner, like a shadow thrown by his father. Italian basketball cognoscenti still remember Kobe shooting around during halftime and being shooed off the court as his father's games were resuming. "The crowd would be cheering me," Kobe says. "I loved it."

"Sure, we were in Italy, but he was around basketball all the time, playing against older guys," Joe says. "He was always wanting to play my teammates, and, you know, the older guys, they would pretend that they were falling down."

"I used to set them up," Kobe says. "I'd say, 'Come on, you're playing a little kid.' Then it would come to game point, and they'd start getting serious, and I knew I had them. My father would be on the sideline talking trash: 'You're gonna let a little 10-year-old bust you up?'"

"I've never seen somebody who can see a move that another guy does and learn it as quickly as he can," Robert Horry, a Lakers forward, says of Kobe. "Usually it takes so long to get a move down, to learn the footwork. Sometimes it takes all summer. But he'll work on it, and two days later you'll see it in his game."

The videotapes used to arrive in Italy every couple of days, like letters from home. Kobe's grandparents would tape the biggest NBA games, as well as TV shows and movies, and Joe would receive tapes of other games from a couple of NBA scouting services to which he subscribed. In all he and Kobe watched the Lakers about 40 times a year. Joe loved seeing the work of an NBA guard his own size. "He comes into the league with all that fancy stuff, and they call it Magic," Joe told reporters near the end of his NBA career. "I've been doing it for years, and they call it 'schoolyard.'"

In a closet in the house the Bryants still own near Philadelphia is the little Lakers jacket that Kobe wore as a baby. Later he graduated to a Lakers letter jacket with leather sleeves. In his room in Italy was a life-sized poster of Magic Johnson. The Lakers were based more than 6,000 miles away, but that only deepened Kobe's appreciation of the way they played. Because the games he saw were on videotape, he didn't see them just once. He memorized them. "He would watch those games like they were a movie, and he knew what the actors were going to say next," says Shaya Bryant, now 20.

The play-by-play analyst for these games was Kobe's father. As they watched tape together, Joe would predict where the ball was headed and why, which made him seem like a wizard to his little boy. Kobe would sit in front of the TV and study what a player did with his shoulders, his feet, his head, as if that were the whole point of watching, to decide how the man was balancing his weight without betraying his intentions. "Genius at first is little more than a great capacity for receiving discipline," wrote the English novelist George Eliot more than a century ago. It may seem as if Kobe was analyzing basketball technique. But as far as he knew, he was just getting to know his heroes.

After watching the tapes over and over, Kobe would go outside, alone, and try to beat the world's best players at their own game, more dependent on his imagination than any kid growing up in America. As a result he gives credit for his fallaway jump shot to Hakeem Olajuwon. "My baseline jumper, I got it from Oscar Robertson," he says. "Oscar liked to use his size against smaller players. That's what I try to do." From Earl (the Pearl) Monroe he realized how to "shake one way, then go back the other way." In Europe Kobe taught himself the fundamentals of basketball. Not until he returned to Philadelphia as an eighth-grader did he develop a crossover dribble and other street moves. "I learned all my dribbling moves from God Shammgod [at summer camps]," Bryant admits happily.

All he had needed, in retrospect, was the firsthand experience of his father, access to videotapes, and a basketball court free of soccer players where he could do his homework. He could not have developed in this way 20 years ago. There would have been no videos in the mail. For the fundamentals he would have had to go to college. If today he plays with a sense of joy, a sincerity, then he learned it from watching Magic Johnson and from hearing the passion of the Italian crowds who sang for his father. "I was like a computer," Bryant says. "I retrieved information to benefit my game." He could have been raised just as successfully in Australia, Iceland, South Africa—just so long as he remained within reach of his father's occasional loose elbow, which kept him from daydreaming too deeply.

"I didn't beat him one-on-one until I was 16," Kobe says. "He was real physical with me. When I was 14 or 15 he started cheating. He'd elbow me in the mouth, rip my lip open. Then my mother would walk out on the court, and the elbows would stop."

In November 1991, Joe and Pam were awakened by one of those dreadful 2 a.m. phone calls. Pam's parents wanted them to hear the shocking news from somebody they trusted. Magic Johnson had just retired from basketball after learning he was HIV positive. Pam and Joe talked it over, and in the morning, without mentioning Johnson's prognosis, they told their 13-year-old son that his idol had been forced into retirement.

They were living in Mulhouse, France, at the time. The boy was crying, and it took all the father's strength not to cry along with him as they took their 45-minute trip across the Swiss border to the international school the children attended.

"I was sad because Kobe was sad," Sharia says. "I never imagined feeling that way about somebody I'd never met. It hurt him as if it was a family member. For a week he was missing meals. It was really, really hard for him."

The Mulhouse club, for which Joe was playing, was shaky financially, and it was also time for the Bryant children to prepare themselves for college in the U.S., so the family moved back home a few weeks later. Kobe turned out to be a much better player than his Italian friends had thought. He launched himself into the American system without hesitation, joining the famed Sonny Hill summer league in Philadelphia. There a counselor scolded him for listing "NBA" as his future career on his application. "The guy said NBA players are one in a million," Bryant recalls. "I said, 'Man, look, I'm going to be that one in a million.' You see Magic, Michael—they made it. What's different about them? The whole thing kind of pissed me off."

No doubt Bryant was lured away from Duke, Michigan, and North Carolina—his three college choices—by the prospect of a millionaire's contract, but the powers of his imagination should not be ignored. Jordan and Johnson were back in the NBA, and in Bryant's mind's eye, they were waving him onto the court. "I wanted to get in the league and play against those guys," he says.

"See, the kids in America, they don't do the work that Kobe did," Johnson says. "That's a problem with the young people now. They don't have the fundamentals." Johnson, now 38 and a Lakers vice president, says he learned about Bryant's special feeling for him "because of his family telling me some things after he joined the Lakers. I also knew because he was always calling here at the office, telling me, 'Let's work out,' or, 'Where are you working out?'"

A lot is made of Bryant's similarity to Jordan. He jumps like Jordan. ("Like Julius, too," his father adds.) He slashes and creates his own shots, much like Jordan (and Julius), and when he needs the extra moment to aim his jump shot, he can hang there, bent forward slightly, as if his shoulder blades have become little wings.

Every now and then, though less often recently, the Lakers turn the Bryant-Jordan comparison around. "Sometimes you say Michael could do things Kobe does," Lakers guard Jon Barry says, "and sometimes it's unanimous that he couldn't."

Sometimes Bryant even sounds like Jordan, answering an interviewer's question the way Jordan would. "That's a by-product of him studying those tapes," says Joe Carbone, Bryant's personal trainer.

Yes, Bryant has a personal trainer, just like Mike. "I just have so much energy," Bryant says. On a game day, early in the morning, he is usually in the gym with Carbone, lifting weights and stretching before meeting his teammates for the shootaround. Some nights he will call Carbone and arrange to meet him at a gym even though the Lakers practiced that afternoon. This summer, regardless of how far the Lakers go in the playoffs, Bryant plans to work out at least five hours a day, half of the time in the weight room, the other half on the basketball floor. "That's when I'm going to pick up my game another five notches," he says.

"It's going to be hard for him to do, because he's not going to get in a lot of quality games over the summer," warns Harris. "What he has to work on is his team game."

Wasn't this the same thing Jordan heard the first seven years of his career? Until June 1991, when he escorted Magic's Lakers out of the NBA Finals, the mantra Jordan heard was that he would never be considered as great a player as Johnson or Bird until he won a championship and proved he could elevate the play of his teammates.

Jordan was stubborn about it. He was the league's top scorer for four consecutive seasons without taking Chicago to the Finals. During the Bulls' five subsequent NBA title runs, he has continued to lead from the front. Bryant's circumstances in Los Angeles are different. By no means is the team built around him, the sixth man; in fact, he says some of his teammates have complained to him that he should be less aggressive on offense.

"If you watch Jordan, you'll see he's not looking for the spectacular play anymore," Harris says. "His highlight films are of him kissing the trophy."

Jordan, meanwhile, has been giving his protégé the opposite advice, as he did after the All-Star Game. "We were talking, waiting to go into the room for interviews," Bryant says. "Michael said, 'It's important for you to stay aggressive. You just have to continue to be aggressive.'"

O'Neal has been offering Bryant similar advice. "When you look at the NBA champions, most of them had a one-two punch," says O'Neal, imagining himself and Bryant as that combination.

This debate—should Bryant be more aggressive or more of a team player?—is going to define his career. He is the Lakers' best one-on-one player, and his ability to create his own shot, as well as dish off to his teammates, will be crucial to the team's success in the playoffs. Bryant is under the most intense scrutiny, knowing that he will receive a large part of the blame if the Lakers lose. He will have to trust his instincts if he is to become the great player who leads his teammates to a title.

"I've been fighting the people around me this year, as far as them questioning my shot selection and how I should adjust to them," he says. He has adjusted somewhat. In a recent road game against the Toronto Raptors he could be seen looking first for the open man, receiving the ball in different positions and passing when he could—things often asked of less gifted players. But he also will have to be stubborn. If he continues to develop his vision, as Johnson believes he will, the Lakers will have to adapt to his strengths, on his terms.

Johnson predicts that Bryant will learn to read the game, to let it flow through him as if he were part of the circuit. "It's going to take him two more years," Johnson says. He has been of this opinion since the conference semifinals last May, when he watched the Lakers' postseason end in Game 5 against the Utah Jazz with four Bryant airballs—one on the final shot of regulation, three more in the disastrous overtime. It was as if Johnson were looking at himself on the TV screen. Twice in his first five years he was blamed for playoff elimination: in the first round against Houston and in the Finals against the Celtics. Each time Johnson recovered to win a championship the following year.

Last May, on the first morning of the Lakers' off-season, a few hours after the team's plane had returned from Utah, Johnson was in the gym at UCLA when who walked in but the 18-year-old himself. "That was just like me," Johnson says. "I loved seeing that from him. That's how I reacted, too. This is where he needs to be."

So it's settled, then. If the rest of us are forever trying to balance our feminine and masculine sides, the great basketball players are trying to bring their Michael side into balance with their Magic side. The Magic side is the one Bryant must develop.

It's certainly there inside him, circulating through him like something passed down by his father. It's the kind of personality trait that can develop only in certain environments. It wouldn't have grown on the East Coast in Joe Bryant's day, it probably wouldn't blossom in Chicago now, and it certainly wasn't going to bloom on the courts of Italy or Lower Merion High, which Bryant led to the Class AAAA Pennsylvania state championship two years ago.

"It could only have happened in L.A. for Magic," Joe Bryant says. "When Kobe was heading out to L.A., I was telling people, 'Look, what Kobe is living is a dream, and hopefully he is going to a place that still believes in dreams.' That's what L.A. is. You go around there, and everyone's searching for that big movie deal or trying to become a star. Then you look at Magic."

"I'm a positive person," Johnson says when you ask him about his health. He has been so aggressive and optimistic in his treatment that doctors can no longer find traces of HIV in his blood (which is not to say that the virus has disappeared). "Kobe's a positive person, too," he continues. "It's like God blessed that trade so that Kobe could come out here and be around a guy who can help him by sitting and watching him every night. I'm going to take care of him, but I'm also going to criticize him when he has to be criticized. Like the other night, when he went out and shot five or six or seven times and wasn't even warmed up. Those are the kinds of things he's going to have to learn if he's going to be what he wants to be, and that's the best ever."

So does a happy ending settle with the evening sun in Los Angeles? In his room overlooking the Pacific, Kobe lies on his bed and watches a videotape of the Lakers, as he has always done. But now, instead of studying Magic, he watches himself. He imagined his future so deeply that he made it come true. Now he studies how he is doing, asks whether he should have rotated defensively or passed to the open man, and sometimes he looks into the corner of the picture, at the big man sitting courtside in the rich suit, at the amazing sight of Magic Johnson watching him play.

Bryant knows that after this game ended, he returned backstage to the very locker that Magic used to occupy like a king on his throne. The Lakers say locker assignments are made by chance, but perhaps an astrologer would argue differently.

When Kobe comes out of his bedroom, it's as if nothing has changed. His parents are still living with him, by his choice; he is still only 19, after all. In fact, apart from the view of the ocean and the expensive fixtures, this might be any one of the places they rented in Italy. He didn't even have to leave home to make his dream come true.

"And if he keeps on growing?" Magic says, because Kobe is now 6'6", an inch taller than he was a year ago. "If he grows to be as tall as Joe?" That will mean he's as tall as Magic. "Then it's just over," Magic says. "Oh, my goodness."

Bryant in the lane against Milwaukee in 1998.

Pairing Bryant with Shaquille O'Neal, signed as a free agent in 1996, had Lakers fans dreaming of a dynasty.

Bryant prepares to take on the SuperSonics at Staples Center in 1999.

In 1999 the Lakers hired head coach Phil Jackson, hoping he could lead Bryant and O'Neal to the NBA Finals. The trio would win three straight championships.

Bryant poses for photographer Walter Iooss Jr. circa 2000.

Bryant takes the ball to the rim against the Nets' Jim McIlvaine in 2000.

Bryant had developed into one of the game's premier guards by the 1999–2000 season.

Excerpted from Sports Illustrated, April 24, 2000

Boy II Man

Erstwhile teen hot dog Kobe Bryant has grown into a consummate team player, which is a big reason the Lakers are huge favorites to win the NBA title

BY PHIL TAYLOR

I had a dream that jealousy
Was a thing of the past.
And we all understood
It's all vanity and it won't last....

—"Visions," a song by Kobe Bryant

Most mornings Kobe Bryant awakens to an ocean view. Before his feet touch the Italian marble floor, he sees the Pacific sparkling outside his bedroom window, a vast blue blanket beneath an endless sky. It's an awesome tableau, yet you suspect that when Bryant gazes at it, there might be something even more spectacular in his mind's eye. He has a way of seeing things that others don't; it's little wonder that his favorite cut from his soon-to-be-released hip-hop album, *K.O.B.E.*, is a wistful tune entitled "Visions."

Bryant's visions have been ridiculed, but that has never deterred him. When he was nine years old and living in Milan, other kids would laugh at his certainty that he would one day be an NBA star. In response he would scribble his name on scraps of paper and hand them to his doubters. "You might want to hold on to this," he would say. Bryant smiles sheepishly at the memory, but he relishes having had the last laugh. He has a way of making cockiness seem lovable, which is one of the keys to his popularity. Why shouldn't he be impressed with himself? If those kids had listened to him, they would have the autograph of a two-time NBA All-Star who, at the tender age of 21, is perhaps the best shooting guard in the league.

Some of Bryant's visions are eerie. When he was chosen 13th in the 1996 NBA Draft by the Charlotte Hornets, who promptly traded him to the Los Angeles Lakers for center Vlade Divac, Kobe told his father, former NBA player Joe (Jelly Bean) Bryant, that someday he'd play for Phil Jackson and his assistant Tex Winter—although Jackson and Winter were coaching the Chicago Bulls at the time. In February

Bryant averaged 22.5 points, 6.3 rebounds, and 4.9 assists in 1999–2000, all career highs.

of last year Kobe phoned Winter to pick his brain about the triangle offense. Not until four months later did the Lakers sign Jackson, who took Winter and the triangle to L.A. "Freaky, isn't it?" Bryant says.

It doesn't take a visionary to see a championship in the Lakers' near future. With a 67–13 record through Sunday, Los Angeles has secured home court advantage throughout the playoffs, and it looms as the kind of prohibitive favorite that few people expected to see so soon after the dissolution of Michael Jordan's Bulls. The Lakers' brilliant year has been largely the result of Jackson's orchestration, Shaquille O'Neal's domination, and Bryant's maturation. These days Bryant is far less inclined than he was as recently as a year ago to indulge in one-on-one forays, which often delighted fans but irritated teammates. Instead he integrates his flights of improvisation into the Los Angeles offense. "He doesn't make his game a personal game anymore," says L.A. forward Rick Fox. "You don't see him doing the things on the floor that used to get him in trouble and get us in trouble."

The 6'7", 210-pound Bryant has also recognized how many ways he can leave his imprint on a game. Not only does he score, but he also initiates the Lakers' attack and has developed into a fierce defensive stopper. "Kobe's a model of what a young player should aspire to be," says Philadelphia 76ers coach Larry Brown. "Year by year he has learned and made his game more solid, and now he's not just a highlight-film guy but an accomplished NBA player."

This has been the best of Bryant's four NBA seasons by any measure: his averages of 22.6 points, 6.2 rebounds, and 4.9 assists through Sunday are career highs. It has also been the season in which he was least noticed. O'Neal is a lock for the MVP award, erasing any doubt that the Lakers are his team. He has been magnanimous in acknowledging Bryant's growth, referring to their partnership as the Combo, but it's clear that anyone who plays with O'Neal is at best the side dish to his entree. Moreover, while the MVP votes are going to Shaq, the style points are going to Toronto Raptors forward Vince Carter, who has passed Bryant in the line of succession to be crowned the next Jordan. Observers have looked closely for any hint of envy from Bryant, but he has shown only one fleeting sign. During a postgame interview on NBC in February, he was asked if the fact that Carter had scored 51 points earlier in the day had spurred him to try to do something equally spectacular. A look of annoyance crossed Bryant's face. "Man," he said, "why do you guys want to ask those questions?" Then he quickly regained his calm and denied any rivalry with Carter.

Otherwise, if Bryant has been annoyed at being overshadowed by O'Neal and Carter, he has hidden it well. "It's actually perfect," he says. "I can learn every facet of the game without everyone analyzing every move I make. It's funny how much people wonder about jealousy. Am I jealous of Shaq? Is he jealous of me? Am I jealous of Vince? I'm not about that. Shaq's been unbelievable, and nobody wants to see him play this way more than I do. Vince? I'm very, very happy for Vince. I love what he's doing."

Bryant and Carter should feel more sympathy than envy for each other, because they are both doomed to be held up to Jordan's standard. Thanks to His Airness, the definition of a superstar has forever changed. It's not enough to be a perennial All-Star, an essential part of a winner, a sneaker-company pitchman. A player can't separate himself from the pack unless he is all those things and more: a corporate mogul, a player in the entertainment world, the leader of a dynasty. Bryant is doing his best to reach the bar Jordan has raised. In December he purchased half-ownership of an Italian basketball team, Olimpia Milano, and he has endorsement deals with Adidas, Mattel, and Sprite, among others, that will generate more annual income than his six-year, $71 million deal with the Lakers. Bryant is also testing the waters in show business with his CD, on which he wrote or cowrote all the songs, and in a deal with Columbia to produce albums for other artists. He has plans for Kobe Family Entertainment, his film production company, to produce movies and sitcoms. When Bryant was a gangly senior at Lower Merion (Pa.) High, many observers feared he was ruining his future by deciding to skip college. In March he was on the cover of *Forbes*, decked out in Armani.

An NBA title would seem to complete the picture of Bryant as an all-around success, the rare young player who has found a balance between sport and celebrity. But to measure up to Jordan, Bryant will have to be the player who leads a team to several championships. He's not in a position to do that with the Lakers. It's hard to be Michael Jordan when your team needs you to be Scottie Pippen.

That's why Bryant's willingness to tone down his game is significant. It doesn't mean, however, that he's content to take a backseat indefinitely. His visions don't include an image of himself as a careerlong second banana. "Somewhere down the line when Shaq comes to me and says, 'Kobe, I don't want to have to put up the big numbers every night, you've got to help me out,' I'll be ready," Bryant says. If O'Neal never makes such a request? "I'm only 21," Bryant says. "When I'm 28, Shaq will be what, 40?" He smiles at his exaggeration, knowing O'Neal will be only 35 then. "Point is, my time will come."

Bryant usually doesn't talk about the future so freely, preferring to concentrate on the present. Ask him what else he envisions for himself five, 10 years from now, and he shakes his head. "I'm not going to tell anybody that," he says. "It's better to keep things like that to yourself. Certain goals you love to share, like winning a championship. Others are to keep yourself interested. I'll just leave it at this: people would be surprised at some of the goals I have."

If you say murder that means I'm a thug poet.
If I say my mind kills that means I'm a thug poet.

"Thug Poet,"
a song by Kobe Bryant

The thug poet sits in the lounge of the Four Seasons Hotel in Vancouver, sipping a virgin piña colada. The only alcohol Bryant drinks is champagne on New Year's Eve and the occasional glass of red wine, a custom to which he was exposed when he lived in Italy while his father played pro ball there. He says Jennifer Love Hewitt is one of his favorite actresses, and his six-bedroom house in Pacific Palisades is within walking distance of his parents' house. This is hardly the profile of a thug, even a poetic one, but that's not the point. Bryant may not be from the streets, but he can speak the street language; he can fit in when he wants to.

Kobe was 13 when his family moved back to the U.S. He'd been born in Philadelphia but moved to Italy when he was six, and he had a hard time assimilating to life in America. The slang baffled him, but he soon picked it up, absorbing it without even realizing he was doing it. He has undergone a similar process as a player in his four years in Los Angeles. He was 18 when he joined the Lakers, a teenager among grown men. "I don't think he was shy, but a certain amount of shock was there," says guard Derek Fisher, who broke in with L.A. the same year that Bryant did. "He was reserved because he wasn't sure how to act. Some guys misinterpreted that to mean he didn't want to hang out with us."

It wasn't until this year that Bryant began to fit in, taking in the occasional movie on the road with teammates, joking around more on the team bus and plane. "It's like he realized that before he could establish himself in this league, he had to establish himself in this room," Fox says, referring to the locker room. Bryant denies that he has tried to open up more to his teammates, but perhaps, as he did after returning to the U.S., he adapted without realizing it. "If you ask me, I acted the same way my first few years, but for some reason the perception is different this year," he says. "If I'm doing something that makes them feel more comfortable around me, then I'm happy about that."

His relationship with O'Neal was the trickiest, but the days when Shaq would publicly express thinly veiled displeasure with Bryant's play are, if not gone, increasingly rare. O'Neal's appearance at Bryant's 21st birthday party last August was the Lakers' equivalent of the end of the cold war, and the two seem at ease with each other on and off the court. "Me and Kobe are cool," says Shaq. "We got to know each other, and we found that there's room in this offense for us both to do our thing."

The triangle helped O'Neal and Bryant learn to coexist. The new offense called for more movement and cutting than the systems used by previous coaches Del Harris and Kurt Rambis. "Basically it was just Shaq in the post and four guys on the perimeter, waiting to see what happened," Bryant says of the old offense. "You couldn't feed off each other in that setup."

"They had to learn that this offense isn't predicated on plays being called for one guy or the other," Jackson says. "It's predicated on how to read the defense and hit the open man, move without the ball and give it up. Sharing breaks down a lot of barriers. There's been the idea in the past on this team that people had different agendas, and the agenda had to come around to 'one for all.' Kobe didn't have a selfish agenda; he just felt that the way he had been playing was the best way he could contribute. Gradually, he's seen there is a different way to contribute that incorporates more of the team."

Bryant believes one reason he and O'Neal struggled to get along is that they are so similar. "We're both attackers," he says. "We both want to get 40 points. I had to figure out how to attack in a different way. I've got it pretty much figured out now—not completely, but almost." And when he figures it out completely? "Then," says Bryant, "I'll be ready for more."

Favorite children's book: *Curious George*, by H.A. Rey. He's always looking for an adventure, just like me.

From Bryant's website

A little-brother analogy is often used to describe Kobe—and not just by his two older sisters, Sharia, age 24, and Shaya, 22. It's cited by others, too, because Kobe is childlike in the best sense, playful, inquisitive, mischievous. A horror movie fan, he has been known to put on a long black trench coat and a mask he got from *Scream* director Wes Craven and hide in the bushes outside his house, popping out to scare his parents and sisters when they come to his door. When he was a boy in Italy, he liked to jump out the family's second-floor window onto the lawn. His jump from high school to the NBA was riskier than those second-story leaps, but his motivation wasn't much different; he wanted to know what would happen when he landed. "I just want to see what I'm capable of," Bryant says. "That's what drives me more than anything: curiosity."

It's curiosity that brings him to longtime Lakers assistant Bill Bertka in search of tapes of great players of the past, such as Pete Maravich. Curiosity led Bryant to seek out exceptional defenders like Eddie Jones, Gary Payton, and Scottie Pippen and ask them for tips on how to improve his own defense. When he was traded to Los Angeles, he immediately called the coaching staff and asked for tapes of guards around the league he would soon be facing.

Bryant learned his lessons well. He has added a new dimension to the Lakers' defense with his ability to smother small, quick guards. His work

A little-brother analogy is often used to describe Kobe—and not just by his two older sisters, Sharia, age 24, and Shaya, 22. It's cited by others, too, because Kobe is childlike in the best sense, playful, inquisitive, mischievous.

against the 76ers' Allen Iverson during an 87–84 win in February was masterly. With a seven-inch height advantage, Bryant barely let Iverson see daylight in the second half, hounding him into 0-of-9 shooting in the fourth quarter and stuffing his final shot. Like Jordan, Bryant uses his defensive prowess to exact revenge on opponents. Larry Hughes of the Golden State Warriors scored 41 points, many of them against Bryant, in a 109–92 L.A. victory on March 9. When the two faced each other again on March 22, Bryant was determined to make Hughes pay for his impudence. He attached himself to Hughes during the first quarter, blocking two of his shots and harassing him into missing six of seven attempts. Meanwhile, Bryant picked up 18 points and four assists. The game was such a blowout—the Lakers won 119–96—that Bryant didn't play enough to torture Hughes further. "I told Phil I wished we had kept the game closer so I could have stayed out there," he says.

Given that kind of performance, it's no wonder that Bryant is curious, above all, about his gifts. He talks about his ability as if it were an object, something to examine from every angle. "I've decided to take my talents to the NBA" is how he began the press conference in which he announced he would bypass college. Now he says, "People say I've made it, but I haven't come close to being where I want to be. It intrigues me to see how far I can go with this thing."

It's hard to blame him, because he hasn't had the freedom that young stars often have. Think of it this way: Bryant never got to sow his oats, at least not many, as a young player. He never went to college and dribbled rings around a future chemical engineer from Drexel. He doesn't seem to have missed that, judging from his incredulous look when he's asked if he regrets never having played in the NCAA tournament. "I get to play with and against the best players in the world," he says. "Why would I feel I missed anything?"

Bryant seems unlikely to become some malcontent consumed by his ego or by jealousy, but he may be consumed by his curiosity. The Lakers have a bright student on their hands who needs to be constantly challenged, and as they move toward what seems to be an inevitable championship, they would be wise to begin planning his next lesson. ●

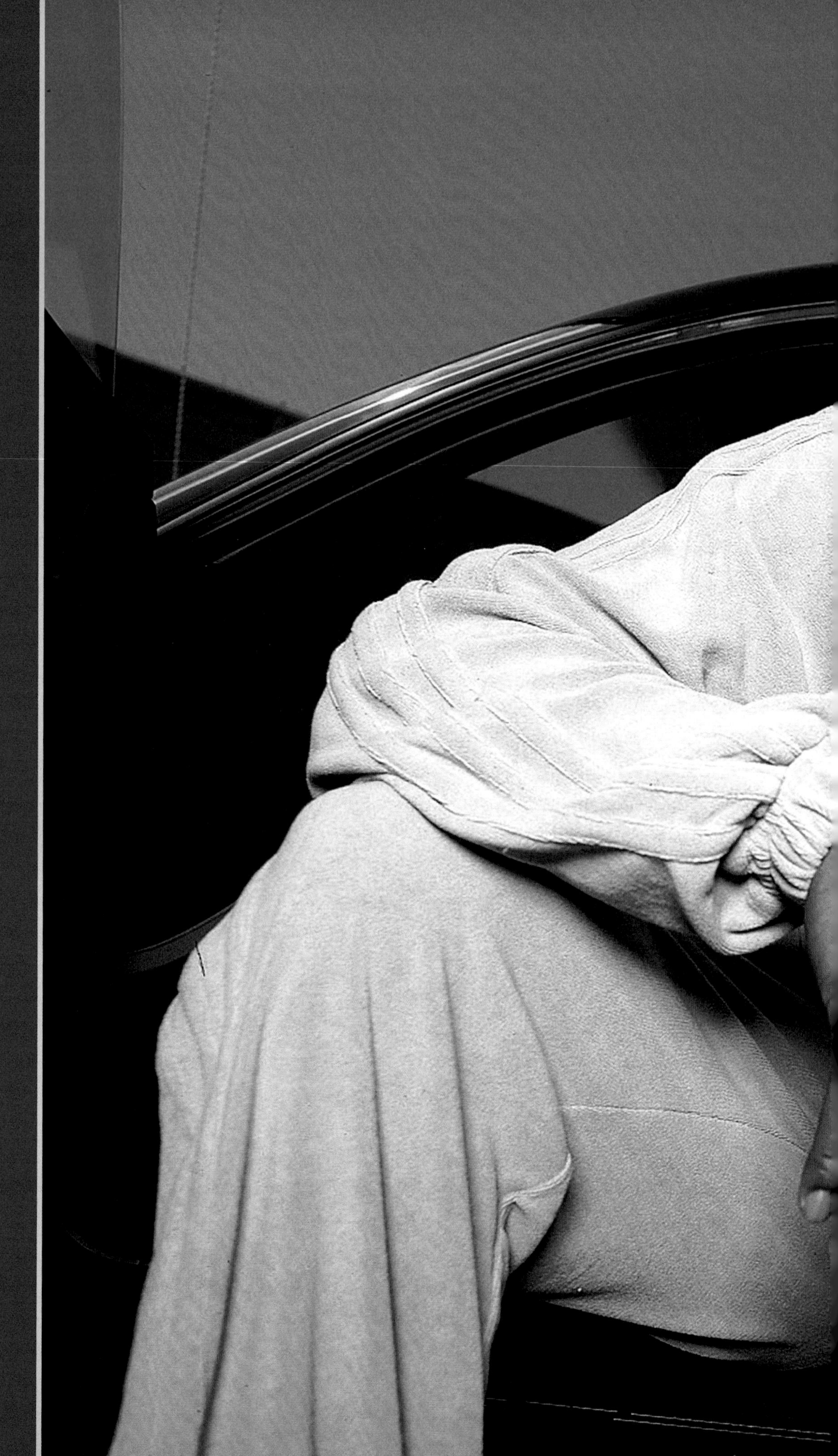

With wealth, stardom, and a piece of an Italian hoops team, Bryant had just about all a 21-year-old could want.

adidas

Bryant shoots against the Pacers in Game 4 of the NBA Finals in 2000.

Champions! Bryant and O'Neal celebrate their first title after beating the Pacers in the NBA Finals in 2000.

Bryant cradles the Larry O'Brien trophy as O'Neal holds the NBA Finals MVP award after defeating the Pacers in Game 6.

NBA FINALS
LAKERS
34

THE SUPERSTAR

Bryant soars against the 76ers in 2000.

Chapter 2

Bryant at Angels Gate Park in San Pedro, California, in 2001.

adidas

COMING UP LATER...
TBS NBA TUESDAY
Game 2 - Wizards vs Lakers

Bryant watches himself on television in the players' lounge in Los Angeles in 2002.

Excerpted from Sports Illustrated, June 25, 2001

Double Dip

Just one question remains for the Lakers after their second straight title: Can their stars stay aligned long enough to seize a third?

BY PHIL TAYLOR

Shaquille O'Neal strolled down a hallway of the First Union Center in Philadelphia last Friday night carrying his Finals MVP trophy and leaving the scent of Dom Pérignon in his wake. "Smell that?" he said. "That's what winning smells like."

He ducked as he entered a makeshift television studio, where his purple-and-gold Los Angeles Lakers jersey hung on a blue curtain next to Philadelphia 76ers star Allen Iverson's. As Shaq deadpanned his way through the interview, Kobe Bryant walked onto the set to await his turn before the camera. With a garish Lakers leather jacket over his uniform and his championship cap askew, Bryant bobbed his head happily as he hummed to himself and cradled the championship trophy, looking like a little boy who had finally gotten the present he'd always wanted.

When O'Neal finished his interview, he saw Bryant standing in the wings, and both men put their hardware down to high-five and embrace. Then, as Shaq exited and Bryant took his place in front of the camera, a member of the TV crew took down the O'Neal jersey from the curtain, revealing Bryant's number 8 uniform hanging behind it. In an instant Shaq's room had turned into Kobe's.

The Lakers wrapped up their second straight NBA title with the closest thing to a perfect postseason the league has ever known, largely because they made a series of similarly deft transitions. They went back and forth during the playoffs, from O'Neal's team to Bryant's and from Bryant's to O'Neal's, without missing a beat—and nearly without being beaten. The 108–96 victory over the noble but overmatched Sixers in Game 5, which wrapped up the championship, was L.A.'s 23rd in 24 games dating back to the regular season, and only Philadelphia's overtime win in Game 1 at the Staples Center kept the Lakers from becoming the first champion to complete an undefeated postseason. "It's especially satisfying to know that we didn't just win, we dominated," says Los Angeles forward Rick Fox. "We made the regular season harder than it had to be with our internal problems, but once we found ourselves, there was no stopping this team."

Sports Illustrated

SPECIAL REPORT
College Football's
Great Recruiting Scam

Together Again

But where do Shaq and Kobe go from here?

JUNE 25, 2001
www.cnnsi.com

Although the Lakers weren't as spectacular in the Finals as they had been in the first three rounds of the playoffs, their dismantling of the Sixers, especially in Philadelphia, was in its own way equally impressive. The three road victories proved that they could grind it out, that in a series billed as Sixers guts against Lakers glitz, L.A. had both. O'Neal, who averaged 33.0 points, 15.8 rebounds, and 4.8 assists in the series, laid waste to the 76ers when they didn't double-team him—Philadelphia center Dikembe Mutombo took more shots to the jaw, courtesy of Shaq, than a bad prizefighter—and passed beautifully out of the pivot when they did. With a pair of championship rings at age 29, O'Neal has the jewelry, the longevity, and the talent to join Bill Russell, Wilt Chamberlain, and Kareem Abdul-Jabbar on the shortlist of the greatest centers of all time. "I have never seen a better player," says Larry Brown, Philly's 61-year-old coach.

The Finals belonged to O'Neal much as the Western Conference finals against the San Antonio Spurs had belonged to Bryant. Against the Sixers, Bryant found little room to make his acrobatic forays to the rim, so he played with admirable restraint yet still stuffed his stat line: 24.6 points, 7.0 rebounds, and 5.8 assists per game. The less-celebrated Lakers, particularly Fox, guard Derek Fisher, and forward Robert Horry, took turns demoralizing Philadelphia with three-pointers, and L.A.'s underrated defense made certain that Iverson, who shot only 40.7% in the series, rarely had a view of the basket that wasn't obstructed by at least one outstretched hand. "It's hard to find a single area where they didn't play well," Philly guard Eric Snow said after Game 5. "This is their second championship, and I'm sure they're thinking that it's not their last one."

It is a measure of how limitless the possibilities seem that Bryant, who as a rookie four years ago brashly declared that the Lakers would win 10 titles during his career, was asked during the championship celebration whether he'd like to amend that prediction...upward. He said he'd let his estimate stand.

"I'm greedy," O'Neal says. "I'm very greedy." That greed seems to have been passed on to his teammates. The 15–1 postseason record isn't only a pretty number for the record books, it's also an indication that the Lakers never lost their appetite, even when they had all but devoured the opposition. In each of their four chances to close out a series, they eliminated the opponent with the cold-blooded efficiency that only great teams consistently muster. "If they're not a great team," Sixers forward George Lynch said after Game 5, "then I don't want to run into one that is."

"People think we hate each other," O'Neal says of his relationship with Bryant. "If we did, we never could have done this two years in a row."

It's no secret that the Lakers' chances of building a dynasty rest on how long this era of good feeling between O'Neal and Bryant lasts. Even in the postclincher giddiness it was hard to find anyone in the Los Angeles locker room who felt sure the two stars had resolved the differences between them, which had fractured the team during most of the regular season. "Hopeful, yes; certain, no," Fox said. "I think it helps that they've seen once again how much we can accomplish when we're all on the same page. But Shaq and Kobe are two strong-willed guys, and there are no guarantees."

Even on the brink of the title, Bryant could muster little more than cautious optimism. "If you look at the teams that have won championships, a lot of them go through some adversity in the regular season," he said the day before Game 5. "We came through it this year even stronger than we were. So I don't see [tension on the team] being a threat at all. But I'll let you know in October." Bryant seemed to be only half joking when he said of his partnership with O'Neal, "We're happy—until next January when people start talking about trading one of us."

The Bryant-O'Neal rift may be a chronic condition, but it's one that the Lakers can probably live with if it's monitored and managed. Former team president Jerry West, the franchise's Obi-Wan Kenobi, will no doubt have more meetings with Bryant like the one they had in March, when he invited Bryant and his agent, Arn Tellem, to his home for a spaghetti dinner and wound up counseling Kobe for four hours on how to adjust his game to work more smoothly with O'Neal's. Similarly, Shaq is sure to have more phone conversations with West like the ones they had this season, in which West reminded him that because of Bryant's youth (he's 22) and still-evolving talents, playing with him would require extra patience. It was telling that O'Neal and Bryant both thanked West publicly during the championship celebration without being asked about him. "He was a big part of the success we had this year," O'Neal said. "A huge part."

The distance between Bryant and the rest of his teammates may also threaten the Lakers' chemistry. Toward the end of last season Bryant began to overcome his tendency to withdraw socially, though some Lakers say he reverted to his old ways this year, curling up with his headphones on team flights while other players played cards or talked. Then on a flight during the team's last road trip of the regular season, Bryant put down the headphones and joined in. "It was a small thing," says guard Brian Shaw, "but it meant a lot."

Bryant downplays the significance of that gesture. "I love these guys," he says. "I don't think I've done anything different or made any changes in the way I am. But if guys feel more comfortable around me than they once did, that's great."

O'Neal and Bryant are as comfortable around each other as they probably ever will be. Although they are not close friends, their differences have always been more professional than personal, each believing he should be the first option in the offense. They sometimes try too hard to show that there's no animosity between them, with displays of affection in front of the cameras that feel forced, but they can be genuinely friendly in private moments. Before an April game in Boston they were talking near the locker room, behind a partially closed door, unaware that anyone could see them. O'Neal leaned over, Bryant whispered something in his ear, and they fell against each other, laughing. "People think we hate each other," O'Neal says. "We don't hate each other. If we did, we never could have done this two years in a row."

It's possible that the Lakers' rocky regular season was humbling enough to help them avoid falling into the same traps in the future. "We thought we could take shortcuts because we were better than everyone else," Fisher says.

Although O'Neal was still the centerpiece of the Lakers offense, Bryant elevated his game in the NBA Finals against the 76ers in 2001.

"I think that's where a lot of the bickering came from. Kobe probably thought, Hey, I did it Shaq's way last year and we won, so now let's see if we can win my way. Then you had Shaq thinking, If Kobe's going to do it his way and leave me out, then I'm not going to play into that and help him. Phil and the rest of us were saying, What the hell is going on? I thought we had this hashed out last year. I guess we didn't appreciate what we had until we admitted to ourselves that if we didn't get it together, we were going to lose our championship and possibly our whole team."

Even if the Lakers have to relearn some of the same lessons every season, they'll surely remember that it's not necessary for their two leading men to be best friends in order to win. Late last Friday night Bryant was still clutching the championship trophy when he boarded the team bus back to the hotel. He walked down the aisle past guard Ron Harper, who was puffing on a stogie, past other teammates sipping beer and chatting on their cell phones, without a word to any of them. He made his way to the last row, where there were seats on only one side of the aisle, then placed the trophy on the window seat and settled down next to it, making it impossible for anyone to sit beside him. His cap pulled low on his forehead, he stared out the window before closing his eyes for a few seconds.

Moments later, O'Neal boarded the bus, still carrying his MVP trophy. He walked to the back, jawing with teammates along the way, and flopped into a seat one row in front of Bryant and across the aisle. The two stars acknowledged each other with a nod and a few words, then Bryant went back to looking out the window on one side of the bus while O'Neal mugged for a camera crew outside the other. The bus pulled away with Shaq and Kobe facing in opposite directions and sharing very little, except the spoils of victory.

During the 2000–01 playoffs, Bryant averaged 29.4 points, 7.3 rebounds, and 6.1 assists per game.

Shaquille O'Neal declared Bryant the best player in the league as the Lakers won their second title in a row.

Bryant reads a newspaper on the team plane as forward Samaki Walker looks over his shoulder in 2002.

OMELET 2.39
BISCUIT
with EGG 1.89
with EGG 1.89
DELUXE 2.89
with SAUSAGE 2.09
with CREAM CHEESE 1.69
BEVERAGES
SMALL
LARGE
SHAKE
ORANGE JUICE
COFFEE/TEA
HOT CHOCOLATE
MEDIUM
SUPER SIZE
SIDE ITEMS
HASH BROWNS
CINNAMON ROLL
Campbell's Soups
You'll be hooked.
Fish Tenders
Salads
NEW! SIZE!

Bryant is treated like the superstar he had become by the staff at a McDonald's in 2002.

Looking to three-peat, Bryant and the Lakers met the Nets in the NBA Finals in 2002.

Bryant averaged 26.8 points, scoring a quarter of the Lakers' points in the series, as they won their third straight championship. He became the youngest player to win three championships in NBA history.

Bryant and O'Neal celebrate their three-peat. It would be the last championship the pair would win together.

Bryant on Sixth Avenue in New York City in 2002.

Excerpted from Sports Illustrated, March 3, 2003

Roll of a Lifetime

Pouring in points by the score and leading the Lakers back into contention, Kobe Bryant is following a master plan he devised as a teen

BY CHRIS BALLARD

In this age of inflated expectations, what if, for once, we did believe the hype? What if the image brokers were right seven years ago when they anointed a skinny high school senior with a shorn head as the next big thing?

What if things that seemed absurdly premature at the time—the NBA's full-page All-Star Game ad featuring the teenager opposite Michael Jordan; the grandiose pronouncements from every pundit with a word processor—turn out to have been prophetic?

That's exactly what's happened in the case of Kobe Bryant, which helps explain why Trail Blazers coach Maurice Cheeks could honestly say last Friday that Portland's defense on Bryant "was pretty good overall," even though he'd exploded for 40 points in a 92–84 Lakers victory. It's tough to cover a guy when, as Scottie Pippen says, "he not only takes tough shots but seems to make them all."

Ask Yao Ming about it. At week's end Bryant had scored 40 or more in nine straight games and 35 or more in 13 straight, a run eclipsed only by Wilt Chamberlain. Midway through this surreal scoring streak, Bryant drove baseline during a 106–99 double-overtime win over the Houston Rockets and rose up over seven and a half feet of human scaffolding for a one-handed jam so fierce that Yao would later say, "Please do not ask me about something so humiliating to my face." Not that Bryant is limited to slashing: in a 93–87 win at Utah a day later, he was hindered by a sore right knee but still went for 40 while making only one layup and nary a dunk. It was a resplendent performance so full of crazy fadeaways, pirouettes, and double-pump leaners that the Jazz fans, who had booed Bryant throughout the game, were chanting "Ko-BEE! Ko-BEE!" by the end.

The numbers are astounding: During those 13 games Bryant averaged 42.4 points, shooting 48.7% from the field and 45.5% from beyond the arc. He scored more points during the streak than every other Laker except Shaquille O'Neal and guard Derek Fisher had over the course of

PETER KING REPORTS FROM THE NFL COMBINE

Sports Illustrated

BEYOND LEBRON

The Next Sports Prodigies

FREDDY ADU Soccer • JOSÉ REYES Baseball • DARKO MILICIC Basketball

Kobe's Run

13 GAMES, 551 POINTS

PLUS

"KOBE IS BETTER THAN MICHAEL"

HERESY FROM RICK REILLY

MARCH 3, 2003 www.si.com
AOL Keyword: Sports Illustrated

the entire season. And those points have come when the Lakers needed them most: with O'Neal in and out of the lineup because of toe and knee injuries, and with a playoff berth on the line. After a 106–101 win over the Seattle SuperSonics on Sunday, in which Kobe scored 41, L.A. was 30–25 and in the seventh spot in the Western Conference, having gone 11–2 since coach Phil Jackson asked Bryant to be more aggressive. O'Neal speaks for many in the league when he says, "Kobe Bryant is the MVP." Then, speaking only for himself, Shaq adds, "He's the gunnery sergeant, and I'm the Big Dog."

The story behind the 24-year-old Bryant's ascent from skinny teen to MVP candidate is one that LeBron James and other heavily hyped phenoms would be wise to heed. Talk to Bryant about basketball long enough, and he can sound like a self-help guru, the Deepak Chopra of the drop step, going on about staying focused and maximizing potential. As tempting as it is to dismiss this as new-age hoops hooey, in the case of Kobe, it works. "It was like he was put on earth to be a great basketball player, and everything that he does is dedicated to becoming that," says Lakers guard Brian Shaw, a 14-year veteran who played with Bryant's father, Joe, in Italy and has known Kobe since he was nine. "The only guy I've been around with that kind of work ethic is Larry Bird."

Work ethic? While attending Lower Merion (Pa.) High, Bryant would get up at 5 a.m. to work out. Then he'd stay for two hours after practice, refining his game. He bragged to friends that he'd go straight to the NBA and that he'd be an All-Star within two years. Cocky? Very. Was he right? Yes.

After that second season, a point at which most 20-year-olds might see fit to enjoy their newfound wealth and adoration, Bryant spent a summer reworking his game. Instead of playing pickup ball, he watched boxes of videotape, pored over Dean Smith's *Basketball: Multiple Offense and Defense*, and practiced. By himself. In a gym with chairs set up to simulate defenders. He remembers a reporter asking when he was going to flame out and fade away, like another Harold Miner. "People didn't know that I was getting up at six and going to the gym and working for eight hours," Bryant says. "They didn't realize that I wasn't planning on going anywhere. I'd worked too hard."

The story behind the 24-year-old Bryant's ascent from skinny teen to MVP candidate is one that LeBron James and other heavily hyped phenoms would be wise to heed. Talk to Bryant about basketball long enough, and he can sound like a self-help guru, the Deepak Chopra of the drop step, going on about staying focused and maximizing potential.

Bryant was on fire in February 2003, scoring 40 or more points in nine consecutive games and averaging 40.6 for the month.

Bryant memorably dunked over Yao Ming in February 2003. Later, the Rockets center said, "Please do not ask me about something so humiliating to my face."

But as Bryant learned, it takes more than hard work to gain your teammates' trust. Early in his career he was aloof, and he didn't help matters by refusing to concede that he occasionally shot too much. "When I first ran into Kobe, I was amazed at how isolated he was," says Jackson. "That's been the biggest improvement in the last three years: his ability to communicate."

Part of that is simply a matter of age. As Shaw puts it, "Nobody was going to listen to him when he was 18, 19 years old. He didn't have enough NBA experience, or even life experience. We all had wives and kids, and he hadn't even gone to college." Bryant is still not a vocal leader, but he has made a conscious effort to relate better to teammates. He dispenses pointers and puts his arm around players. Two weeks ago, against the Knicks, he pulled aside reserve center Stanislav Medvedenko. "I scolded him pretty hard because I felt like he wasn't ready to play, but I let him know it wasn't personal," says Bryant. "The difference is, a few years ago I would have said something negative and moved on. I wasn't aware of the human side of a person."

For a man who'd spent his life obsessively focused on his career, it took a while to realize the obvious. The catalyst? "Being married kind of forces you to be a better communicator," says a sheepish Bryant, whose wife of 1½ years, Vanessa, had their first child, Natalia, last month. "I'm a better listener now, that's for sure."

Bryant's emotional maturity has been mirrored by advances on the court. Helped in part by the 15 pounds of muscle he added in the off-season, he has become a better rebounder, a better finisher, and, most important, a better long-range marksman. A career 31.4% three-point shooter before this season, he was shooting 38.5% at week's end. "It's the most improved part of his game," says Lakers forward Rick Fox. "He has better balance. It's almost as if he's at peace before he shoots."

All this only fuels what is already the 6'7" Bryant's greatest asset: his hypercompetitiveness. Even in practice, if he loses a game of one-on-one or a shooting contest, "he immediately wants to play you again after practice," says Shaw. At times this can backfire on him, though. On Sunday night against Seattle, Bryant had 39 points with four minutes to play. In his quest to reach 40, he forced and missed six shots before sinking two free throws with 23 seconds left. After the game, Bryant apologized to his teammates for taking them out of the offense. It wasn't the streak that drove him, he explained to reporters, but the challenge. "There are these five guys, and they're all trying to stop me from scoring one basket," he said, his eyes opening wide. Walking out to his car a short while later, he saw Sonics guard Brent Barry, who smiled and said, "Ho-hum, just another 40." Bryant returned the smile and said, "Yeah, but you made me work for it, man."

Sunday's ending aside, Bryant's recent scoring splurge has been a matter of necessity, not ego, all in the service of winning. That has silenced—for now, at least—the critics who accused him of being selfish, especially early this season when the Lakers got off to a 3–9 start while O'Neal recovered from toe surgery. Even assistant coach Tex Winter, who is a notorious crank on such matters, approves of Kobe's recent fusillade. "Normally we don't like him taking shots under such duress," says Winter. "But he's got such a hot hand that you have to ride it." That's high praise, coming from the man who invented the triangle, an offense designed to promote sharing.

So there you have it, LeBron: the road map from phenom to superstar. You merely have to work harder and longer than anyone else, stay confident, marry a woman who makes you a better person, win over your critics, and, somewhere along the way, learn to score like Wilt Chamberlain. No problem. Now get to it.

Bryant scores against Portland during his streak of 40-plus-point games.

LAKERS
8
BLAZERS
1
6
STAPLES
10:24
14
MGD
GENUINE DRAFT
SHARP
LG

Excerpted from Sports Illustrated, March 3, 2003

Like Mike, Or Even Better

Why can't America realize that falling in love with Kobe doesn't mean breaking up with Michael?

BY RICK REILLY

Basketball fans can be dumber than a box of anvils. "Where will we ever find another Michael Jordan?" they wail. If they'd only stop whining, they'd see someone right under their noses who could wind up better than Jordan.

I know, I know. I'm on crack. I'm a twit. I sleep with farm animals. But just listen for a second.

At 24, Kobe Bryant has three rings. At that age, Jordan had zero. At 24, Kobe has better all-around court sense, a better J, and, unthinkably, even more madly creative midair Gumbyness than Jordan did. At 24, Kobe is hitting 38.5% of his treys; Jordan was shooting 18%. Over the last four weeks Kobe was on a mind-warping, pupil-popping, scorched-earth tear during which he scored 35 or more points in 13 straight games. Jordan hadn't done that at 24. Come to think of it, Jordan still hasn't done that.

"He's the best player in the game right now," Utah guard Mark Jackson said last week, after Kobe went for 40 points to help the Shaqless Lakers beat the Jazz. "He's playing basketball that's as good as I've seen in my career." Of course, Jackson's only been in the league for 16 years.

So why can't America embrace Kobe and his ozone-piercing potential? Why can't they realize that falling in love with Kobe doesn't mean breaking up with Michael? I mean, what's not to love?

Here's a young man who speaks fluent Italian, is married and has a child, and never shows up in the back of a squad car. Here's a pro who works out eight hours a day in the off-season, who one summer wouldn't go home until he'd made 1,000 jumpers a day. Here's a young god who's runway handsome, *GQ* cool, and Eagle Scout nice.

In Game 4 of the Western Conference semifinals in San Antonio last May, he blew up for 12 points in the fourth quarter to beat the Spurs. He was seconds from going live with NBC when he saw a small boy crying over the loss. He left the interviewer, went over, and hugged the kid. Yet all anybody wants to do is line him up against Jordan and make sure he loses. Kobe's getting sick of it, and I don't blame him.

"People want to compare me with Michael in his prime," he says, "and that's unfair. I don't think I'm in my prime yet. I think a player's prime is, like, 26 to 30. I'm only 24. But that's all they want to talk about. They're not saying, 'Kobe worked really hard at getting better at this.' Or, 'This is what I appreciate about Kobe.' It's always what I do in relation to Michael. Like, they say my competitiveness came from watching Michael. It never crossed their minds that I've been like this since I was five."

Savor this kid. Wallow in his starshine. Be stupefied, mind-boggled, brain-bent. He's writing his legend right under our noses. Beats his man left-hand dribble, skies baseline, and flushes over Yao Ming? Catches a long outlet, goes behind his back to lose a Denver Nugget, and 360 slams? Driving the baseline, takes off outside the paint, loses Latrell Sprewell in midair, and reverse dunks on the far side of the rim? And that's just in the last three weeks.

You want to argue? Bring it.

Jordan never had a Shaq. True, and Kobe never had a Hall of Fame swingman like Scottie Pippen. Or a rebound-munching forward as Dennis Rodman was in his prime. You think he wouldn't be handy to have around? Why, yes, Dennis, I would like to shoot again, thanks!

Jordan won 10 scoring titles. Kobe's got zilch. I watched Kobe score 56 in three quarters against Memphis last season—the man could win a scoring title wearing Muppet slippers. But many nights he has to put his ego in a jar to keep Shaq-Fu happy and well-fed with points. Plus, Kobe has the burden of handling the rock an awful lot—more than Jordan. "I'm not saying it's harder," says Kobe, "but it consumes a lot more energy, having those little guards crawling on you all the time. It's definitely more running."

Kobe doesn't D-up like Jordan. True, but he's learning. He's increased his steals from 1.48 a game last season to 2.24 this season. He's averaging a career-best 7.0 rebounds, too. Jordan only beat that once. He's got the Bally's body at 24 that Jordan didn't build until he was 30.

I don't see six rings on Kobe's fingers. Let's say Kobe retires when Jordan will, at 40. That means he'd play 23 seasons. You think Kobe can't get four more rings in the next 16 seasons? "Seven rings, eight rings, nine rings," Kobe says, "I don't care. I just want to win. Every year."

Yeah, well, the world will never love Kobe as much as Jordan. True, but maybe that's because Michael came first. If the order had been reversed, would Kobe have the IMAX movies, the jingles, and the shoes? Would Michael be the one wearing Kobe's throwback at the All-Star Game?

They said nobody would ever punk Ruth's numbers. Then came Aaron. They said nobody would go lower than Nicklaus. Then came Tiger. Just roll the possibility around on your tongue for a second: Kobe Bryant could end up the greatest player in NBA history.

"Ooh," says Kobe, "you just gave me goose bumps."

The feeling is mutual.

Bryant holds the ball against Toronto's Vince Carter, another player often thought of at the time as the "next Jordan."

Though they'd won three championships as teammates, the relationship between Bryant and O'Neal was always under scrutiny.

THE FALLEN STAR

Chapter 3

Bryant on the bench with Gary Payton before a game against the Spurs in 2004. Payton and fellow star Karl Malone were brought to L.A. to help the Lakers win another title; the gambit failed.

Excerpted from Sports Illustrated, July 28, 2003

The Dark Side of a Star

Kobe Bryant's carefully cultivated image has been badly stained by his admission of adultery, and a charge of sexual assault

BY JACK McCALLUM

If Kobe Bryant had not yet become the next Michael Jordan he was most assuredly not Allen Iverson, and for that most NBA fans were grateful and bestowed on him much love. The Los Angeles Lakers' 24-year-old superstar cooperated with the media after games, smiled warmly and was polite to fans, and rarely mouthed off to opponents or referees.

Bryant maximized his breathtaking talent on the court and his marketing power off it, but when the cameras were off he provided only glimpses of himself, shutting out the world behind designer shades, an often haughty demeanor, and his insistence that his private life was just that. We knew only as much about this 6'7" child of fortune as he wanted us to know.

That is no longer the case.

By his own admission, Bryant, the married father of a six-month-old daughter, is an adulterer. And in the view of district attorney Mark Hurlbert and other Eagle County, Colo., authorities he is something far worse: a felon who around midnight on June 30 sexually assaulted a 19-year-old woman in a hotel room, a charge that Bryant forcefully denies, and one that carries a prison sentence of four years to life.

It seems naive in the extreme to profess amazement that a professional athlete might have extramarital sex, given the privileges of the lifestyle, the ease with which the stars attract women, and the fact that so many high-profile males (a president, for one) have been unfaithful. While some who never bought into Bryant's squeaky-clean persona were still surprised by the allegation of violence, others have long believed he has a darker side. The excavation of his life and character has begun.

"Kobe is an extremely cold and calculating man," says a source close to Bryant in the Lakers' organization who requested anonymity. But the Bryant on display at a press conference last Friday at the Staples Center appeared to be vulnerable and apprehensive, even during those moments when he insisted that the sex in the

Kobe Bryant sheds a tear as he proclaimed his innocence of the sexual assault charges filed by the district attorney of Eagle, Colorado, for the alleged rape of a 19-year-old Colorado woman.

Colorado hotel room was consensual. Bryant prides himself on his steely composure, but he had to choke back tears and, before 100 reporters, including one from *Celebrity Justice*, admit in a quavering voice that he had strayed. "I sit here before you guys furious at myself, disgusted at myself for making the mistake of adultery," Bryant said, shaking his head and pursing his lips, trying to stay in control as his 21-year-old wife, Vanessa, gripped his hand and stared into his eyes.

Bryant is scheduled to be arraigned in Eagle County on Aug. 6, and if the case proceeds, he will probably stand trial in Colorado next year. The court of public opinion, meanwhile, has already convened. Assuming that Bryant will be clothed in Lakers purple and gold at the start of the 2003–04 season—the NBA has already said he will be allowed to play while the case is pending—he will have to tune out the barbs from fans who have seen him torch their teams over his seven seasons. How he bears up will go a long way toward deciding the fate of a franchise that last Thursday held an upbeat press conference to announce the signing of free agents Karl Malone and Gary Payton, a serendipitous one-two that many believed would return Los Angeles to championship form.

The media affair at the arena 31½ hours later was, by contrast, somber and strange—dramatic because the Bryants' appearance was a surprise, riveting because of the severity of the charges facing Kobe, jarring because of his affirmations of love to his wife ("You're a piece of my heart, you're the air I breathe"). Bryant's lead lawyer, Pamela Mackey, said the evidence pointed to her client's innocence, while L.A. general manager Mitch Kupchak issued a statement of the team's support but did not speak.

As of Monday none of the major companies for which Bryant endorses products (Nike, Coca-Cola, McDonald's, and Spalding) had pulled out of their deals with him—he earns a reported $20 million a year off the court—even though disreputable behavior can result in the cancellation of such contracts. In 1997 Converse terminated its four-year, $32 million deal with Latrell Sprewell after he choked P.J. Carlesimo, his coach with the Golden State Warriors.

Separating fact from fiction is never easy with superstar athletes. Their exploits between the lines make them heroic; their carefully constructed corporate images make them iconic. There is Kobe leading the Lakers to titles in 2000, '01, and '02, then scoring 40-plus points in nine consecutive games last season. There is Kobe, in a McDonald's commercial, stopping at a playground to shoot hoops with kids. There is Kobe, in a spot for Sprite, grunting through a sweat-soaked free-weight workout. For Bryant and the companies trading on him, these images of the man, in effect, become the man himself.

At 10 p.m. on June 30, Bryant, accompanied by three, as of Monday, unidentified men, checked into the Lodge & Spa at Cordillera, a 56-room resort located halfway between the small town of Eagle and the ski resort of Vail. He was scheduled to have arthroscopic surgery on his right knee at the Steadman Hawkins Clinic in Vail the next day. While working at the lodge's front desk, the alleged victim, a receptionist and concierge, reportedly spoke with Bryant. Between 11:13 and midnight she went to his room and stayed for an undetermined length of time. While she was alone with Bryant, the alleged sexual assault occurred.

Bryant's legal team is headed by Mackey, who successfully defended Colorado Avalanche goalie Patrick Roy in a domestic violence charge in 2001, and Hal Haddon, who represented John and Patricia Ramsey in the still unsolved 1996 killing of their daughter, JonBenet. The 34-year-old Hurlbert, a graduate of nearby Summit High who got a law degree at Colorado, tried his biggest case in 2002, when he successfully prosecuted burglar-alarm vendor Charles Garrison for murdering his wife and burying her in their front yard. Hurlbert's handling of a recent sexual assault case came to light in

The Denver Post on Sunday, when an alleged rape victim told the paper that Hurlbert dropped the charges in her case last January, three days before the trial was to have begun. Hurlbert told the *Post* he dismissed the case because he did not believe it was provable; two former deputy district attorneys said they believed that it was.

Last Friday, Hurlbert stood outside the Eagle County Justice Center on a sweltering afternoon, his comments going out to a national TV audience. He emphasized his concern for the alleged victim and said that he had consulted with other prosecutors around the state before deciding that he had sufficient evidence, both physical and testimonial, to accuse a sports superstar—a man who finished behind only Tiger Woods and Michael Jordan in a Burns Sports and Celebrities, Inc., poll ranking athletes as reliable endorsers—of rape. "I have an ethical burden not to prosecute unless I can prove my case beyond a reasonable doubt," he said. "I believe I can."

Since entering the NBA out of Lower Merion (Pa.) High in 1996, Bryant has exhibited a charitable side: He has been involved with the Pediatric AIDS Foundation and the Center for Abused Children. A couple of years ago T.J. Simers, a *Los Angeles Times* sports columnist known for his sarcasm, opined that his daughter could shoot three-pointers better than Bryant, a comment to which Kobe responded with good humor, agreeing to shoot against her for charity. Here's what Simers wrote in his column on Sunday: "I don't write the headlines in this newspaper, but I wouldn't have disagreed with the one on the Page 2 (March 28, 2002) column: THIS IS A GUY THEY CAN BRING HOME TO DADDY."

Among the Lakers, though, Bryant has been viewed as a wondrous talent but an extremely aloof individual who pursued his own agenda, sitting alone in the back of the team bus, Walkman or cell phone pressed to his ear. He frequently travels with his longtime trainer, Joe Carbone, and two or three members of a security team. Bryant's very presence in Colorado demonstrated his autonomy: he had made the appointment for surgery without informing the team.

Bryant faced the media with his wife, Vanessa. It was just the beginning of the media maelstrom.

Bryant's longtime agent, Arn Tellem, typically does not handle his affairs now and would not comment on him. The Tellem associate at SFX Sports who works most extensively with Bryant, Rob Pelinka, referred questions about him to Mackey. However, one source close to SFX calls Bryant "rude and condescending," describes being "horrified at times by how he treated people," and adds that while many clients can be abrasive, Kobe "was among the worst."

For star athletes, every public appearance outside the lines is an encounter between heroes and hero worshipers with potential for exploitation on either side. Lakers coach Phil Jackson said last week that Bryant is "an intelligent young man who learns from mistakes" and that he will "turn this one into a growth situation." Perhaps. Before charges were filed, Bryant defended himself to the *Los Angeles Times*, saying, "You guys know me.... You know I would never do something like that." But only when all the facts are revealed will anyone know who Kobe Bryant really is.

Kobe Bryant stands between his attorneys before Judge Terry Ruckriegle inside the Eagle County Justice Center in May 2003. Bryant pleaded not guilty during proceedings in his sexual abuse case.

BERWOLVES
LAKERS

Karl Malone and Bryant battle Minnesota's Kevin Garnett for a rebound in 2004.

LOS ANGELES
LAKERS
The Finals
DIRECTV
THE HOME DEPOT
McDonald's
BUD LIGHT
Sempra Energy

His trial caused Bryant to miss a number of games, or attend court and travel to play later that night. Still, the Lakers reached the NBA Finals to face the Pistons. Bryant averaged 22.6 points and 4.4 assists on just 35.1% shooting as Detroit upset L.A. in five games.

Excerpted from SPORTS ILLUSTRATED, July 26, 2004

The End

By trading Shaquille O'Neal and keeping Kobe Bryant, the Lakers dropped the curtain on the NBA's most riveting soap opera. (Can you hear the applause all over the West?)

BY JACK McCALLUM

They are at last emancipated from each other after being bound (however tenuously) for eight years, with a continent between them, free to snipe away with impunity. The trading of Shaquille O'Neal to the Heat of Miami (which becomes a new "media mecca," according to Shaq) and the re-signing of free agent Kobe Bryant by the Lakers of Los Angeles (soon to be a lesser media mecca, at least by NBA standards) dominated a momentous off-season in a league that not so long ago didn't even own a hot stove.

But when all the stories about Shaq were written (for local scene, SHAQ IS BIGGEST BIG NAME YET proclaimed the front page of *The Miami Herald* on July 14, followed by a $HAQING UP headline in the business section) and all the denials from Bryant were in ("If [Phil Jackson's] departure had something to do with me, I had no idea" and "People assume I didn't want [Shaq] around. That's not true"), the clear winners after the breakup of this *As the World Turns* team were…the champion Detroit Pistons and the Western Conference (except, of course, the Lakers).

There's no denying the impact O'Neal will have in Miami. Some 400 number 32 jerseys were ordered from the Heat's website in the first two hours they were available. Team president Pat Riley likened the ticket-selling scene at AmericanAirlines Arena last week to the floor of the New York Stock Exchange. Revelers at South Beach were already salivating over the prospect of the Big Buzz making the scene. But having dealt its starting frontcourt (Lamar Odom, Brian Grant, and Caron Butler) plus a No. 1 pick, Miami is far from the favorite in the East. The Heat still needs a frontline player or

TRAINING CAMPS OPEN

HERE COMES THE NFL

CAN THE BENGALS' CARSON PALMER EARN HIS STRIPES? ▸▸

PLUS: Big questions for the Cowboys, Bucs, Eagles, Chiefs and Patriots

Sports Illustrated

TODD HAMILTON WINS THE BRITISH OPEN

Maria Sharapova's Fast Lane

JULY 26, 2004 www.si.com
AOL Keyword: Sports Illustrated

While their separation may have been inevitable, some blamed Bryant for O'Neal's departure from the Lakers.

two, and two-thirds of its payroll now belongs to a 32-year-old podiatric puzzle who will make $58.3 million over the next two years.

As for the Lakers, look for the triangle offense to be replaced by Bryant's "my angle" offense. (Hey, you need to take a lot of shots to earn the maximum, $136.4 million over seven years.) But even if Bryant averages 30 points, the Lakers are no better than the fifth-best team in the West. Take O'Neal out of the conference and every other team gets better—it's that simple.

If Karl Malone returns to L.A., it won't be to the soap opera in which he played a supporting role this past season; then again, it might not be much of anything. Even in this realm of oversized men brazenly pursuing their own agendas, it's hard to fathom the Lakers' implosion. "In the history of the game," said one GM, "there's never been that much turmoil after that much success." Anyone with any sense knows that a team with Shaq and Kobe on the same page (or at least in the same book) and Jackson ruling sagaciously from the sideline should have been practically unbeatable. On some level O'Neal and Bryant knew that as well.

Yet they all went their separate ways: Shaq demanded a trade and Jackson reached a mutual decision with owner Jerry Buss that he would not be offered another contract. Jackson had conceded, publicly at times and much more strongly in private, that his relationship with Bryant was troubled. "They wanted to make some moves to accommodate signing Kobe," he said last week. "We knew they probably wouldn't work if I was coaching the team." Shaq, who has always slyly gotten his point across about Bryant without blasting him directly, said last week, "If you look at all the pieces of the puzzle that are thrown out there and you understand the game and understand the politics, you can put it all together and draw your own conclusions."

Disingenuous doesn't even begin to describe Bryant's reaction to the destruction of what could have been a dynasty. He denied urging

"In the history of the game," said one GM, "there's never been that much turmoil after that much success."

Buss to get rid of Shaq and Jackson, denied lobbying for the hiring of Duke coach Mike Krzyzewski, and said he was hurt by the accusations that his Machiavellian dealings had broken up the team. Then he admitted that he had called Krzyzewski—Coach K spurned L.A.'s five-year, $40 million offer—and that he did not recommend retaining Jackson to Buss.

But it's not all Bryant's fault. O'Neal's aversion to conditioning (he has missed 15 games in each of the last three seasons) contributed to Bryant's not wanting to play with him, a fact confirmed by multiple Lakers sources. Shaq was also demanding a huge extension that Buss had no desire to grant. And perhaps Jackson realized the time had come to recharge his batteries at his home in Montana, probably to return as a coach (in New York?) or a team president.

The only thing clear about the NBA earthquake that hit L.A. last week is that the fortunes of the purple and gold have declined—even with the return of center Vlade Divac, 36, who on Monday reportedly agreed to a free-agent deal with the Lakers. "It's going to be a struggle for us, an uphill battle," Bryant said last week. And provided he is still plying his chosen trade after the conclusion of his sexual assault trial which begins in Eagle, Colo., on Aug. 27, it will be his struggle, his uphill battle.

The mood in Miami is immeasurably lighter, festive even, befitting the arrival of a supersized celeb in a party-hearty town. As Shaq got prodded and probed and MRI'd in Coral Gables last Thursday, passersby stared into the windows at Doctors Hospital, photographers hid in bushes, and a news helicopter hovered overhead. Before heading to L.A. for the weekend, O'Neal did give South Florida a dose of Shaq-yak. He said that he wants to finish his career in Miami; that he had been thinking about buying a house near there anyway because he likes to take his kids on boat rides in the Atlantic; that facing the Eastern Conference centers, "outside of [Indiana's] Jermaine O'Neal, is not going to be that difficult for me"; and that he sees himself being competitive for five or six more years. "Buy tickets," he told a group of fans, "and be ready to roll."

Yes, it's the summer of Shaq, and the living is easy. But not for Bryant. Between these two superstars, who perhaps flew too high too fast to enjoy the ride, right now it is assuredly less trying to be O'Neal. But judgment day between the lines will come for the Diesel, too, because the Heat didn't acquire him just to sell jerseys or jazz up the scene at Liquid. Together, O'Neal and Bryant prospered, but their partnership could not endure. Will they ever prosper apart?

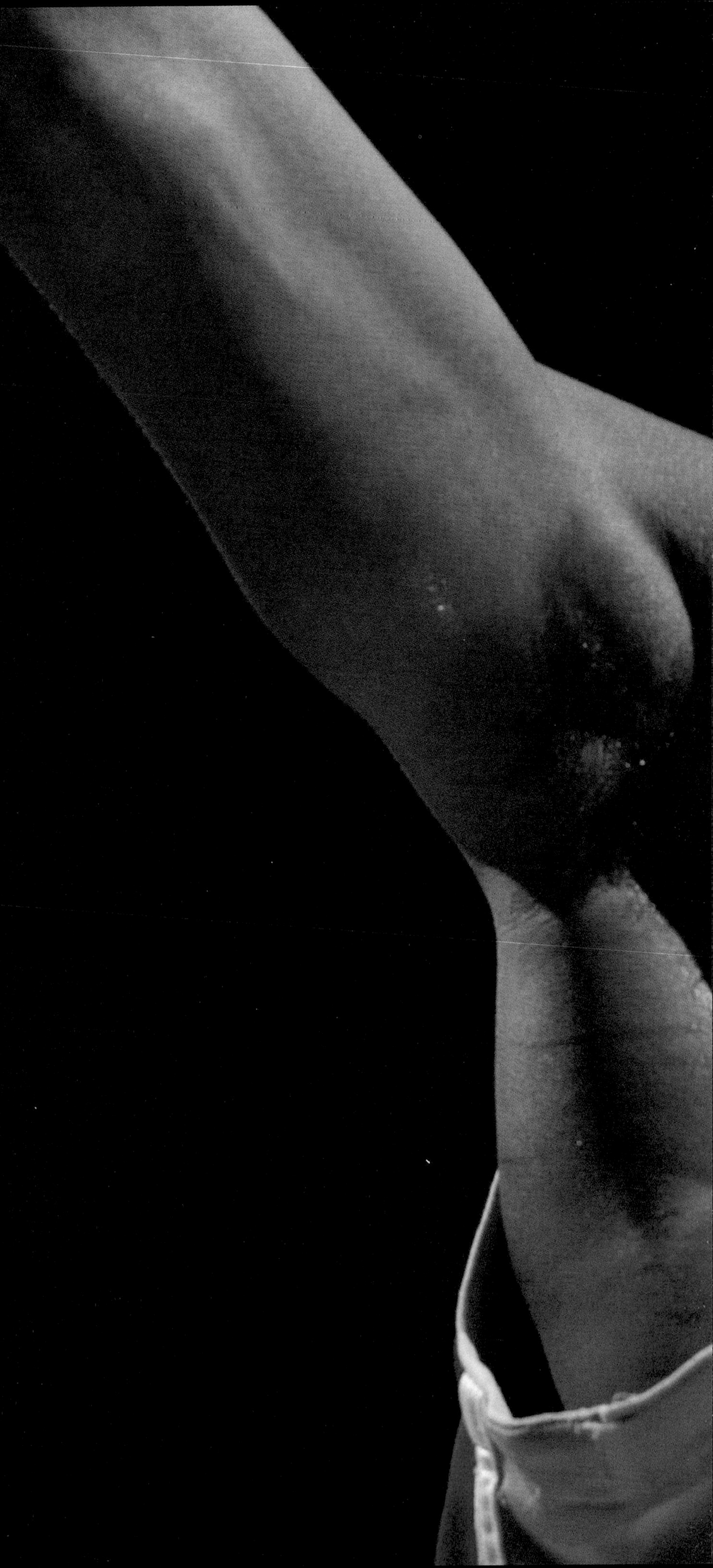

LAKERS

Bryant posts up against Richard Hamilton during the NBA Finals in 2004. The Lakers were upset by the Pistons in five games.

Bryant with daughter Natalia before a game in 2005.

THE BLACK MAMBA

Bryant celebrates a victory against Phoenix in the playoffs in 2006.

Chapter 4

Bryant rises over the Clippers' Sam Cassell early in the 2006 season.

DAKTRONICS
208
TOYOTA
Clippers
42
LAKERS
31

Bryant attacks the rim against Minnesota in 2005, Bryant's second season without Shaquille O'Neal.

FSN WEST 2
LA MIN
8
LAKERS
11

Excerpted from Sports Illustrated, January 30, 2006

Eighty-One

Forget Jordan. Step aside, LeBron. Scoring machine Kobe Bryant had the second-highest point total in NBA history. Now the question is, Can he crack triple digits?

BY JACK McCALLUM

There are no moving pictures of Wilt Chamberlain's 100-point game at the Hershey (Pa.) Sports Arena on March 2, 1962, and so that epic performance has been consigned to the dim mists of history. Like Bigfoot, the Big Dipper stomps along in our collective imagination of that evening, grainy, not quite real.

But then, in living color and looping through 24-hour news channels, came Kobe Bryant and his 81 points. Truly, we can say we've never seen anything like it. On Sunday, Bryant laid four score and one on the Toronto Raptors at Staples Center, where his Los Angeles Lakers overcame an 18-point third-quarter deficit to win 122–104. Nobody besides Wilt has ever racked up more in an NBA game, and the 6'7" Bryant did it with relative economy, making 28 of his 46 shots and 18 of his 20 free throws. (Chamberlain was 37-of-63 from the field, 28-of-32 from the line.) "Eighty-one is 81," marveled New Jersey Nets guard Vince Carter the following day. "I don't care if you're playing summer league, pickup, or PlayStation." Michael Jordan, with whom Bryant is inextricably linked (usually in this sense: Kobe is no Michael) had a career best of 69 points, and for that he needed overtime. Kareem Abdul-Jabbar, the NBA's most prolific scorer, topped out at 55. Bryant got that many in the second half on Sunday.

But what is most notable about Bryant's eruption is that it seemed almost inevitable. In a rout of the Dallas Mavericks on Dec. 20, Bryant had 62 points through three quarters, then sat out the fourth. On Jan. 6, he tattooed the Philadelphia 76ers for 48, winning a duel (and a game) against Allen Iverson. The next night, against the Los Angeles Clippers, he dropped in 50 points, including 40 in the second half. Since his explosion against Dallas, Bryant was averaging 43.4 points at week's end on respectable 46.6% shooting from the floor.

Clearly, something is going on. Bryant will tell you, poker-faced, that he is scoring so

By 2006, the Lakers were fully Bryant's team. He scored 81 points against the Raptors that January.

much—he led the league with 35.9 points per game through Sunday, the highest figure since Jordan's 37.1 in 1986–87—only to increase his team's chances of making the playoffs. (At 22–19, the Lakers were seventh in the Western Conference.) But down deep, fueled by testosterone and pride, Bryant has set out to occupy a place atop the current NBA hierarchy, a spot that, in his mind, he has never reached.

From the moment that Bryant joined the NBA out of Lower Merion (Pa.) High in 1996, his talent stamped him as the heir apparent to Jordan. But few believed he had the maturity to match Jordan on the floor and the charismatic personality to match him off it. When the Lakers won championships in 2000, '01, and '02, Shaquille O'Neal was unquestionably L.A.'s leading man. Bryant's legal troubles stemming from a 2003 rape charge in Colorado brought him down another peg. Coming into this season, Bryant was hardly passé, but neither was he top-of-mind, not with younger superstars like the Cavaliers' LeBron James and the Heat's Dwyane Wade on the rise.

As the season nears the halfway point, however, Kobe has made himself the story in the NBA. "Everybody called every player in the league," says Wade of the 81-point onslaught, "because that's history right there." Not to mention great theater. Last Saturday the 21-year-old James scored 51 to surpass Bryant as the youngest player to reach 5,000 points. So Kobe went out 24 hours later and got his 81, as if to say, LeBron Who?

And now he's reaching back into ancient history. It's difficult to compare Bryant's 81 with the 100 Chamberlain scored as a Philadelphia Warrior. Chamberlain was an imposing 7'1", 270-pound specimen who, while graceful and athletic, physically dominated the opposing center in almost every game. On the night he hit the century mark against the Knicks—heck, on most nights over the first seven years of his career, during which he averaged 39.5 points—his teammates did little else but feed him the ball. And his 100-point night didn't exactly happen under the bright lights.

"I mean, it did happen in Hershey, Pennsylvania," says Lakers coach Phil Jackson. "It was an entirely different atmosphere from getting 81 in a game in Los Angeles, [in] a game where people can double-team you, zone you, trap you, get the ball out of your hands. Players who were at Hershey that night said that the rims were more than forgiving, too. I mean, Wilt, who couldn't shoot free throws for a damn [51.1% for his career], made 28 of 32."

Jackson laughed, then added, "On the other hand, 81 isn't 100."

Bryant, too, didn't have much trouble getting the ball back from his teammates on Sunday night. They may not like him, but they stand in awe (sometimes literally, to the dismay of Jackson, who likes ball movement in his triangle offense) of his ability. But, unlike Chamberlain, Bryant often had to bring up the ball, free himself on screens, squeeze himself between defenders, and dribble this way and that to create space and get off shots. Chamberlain's 100-point night was rather a straight-ahead feast, all roast beef and potatoes; Bryant's 81-point night was a smorgasbord, with six layups or dunks, and 22 jumpers that came from all angles.

Could Kobe hit triple figures? The odds say no. Defenses would do almost anything to prevent it—face-guard him so he couldn't get the ball, put as many as four players on him, dismember him, anything not to become known as *the team that gave up a hundred*. Here was Utah Jazz coach Jerry Sloan, a legendarily tough guy, reflecting on Bryant's achievement the day after: "I wouldn't feel very good about myself if a guy scored a lot of points and I didn't use my fouls to try to stop him." Said Heat forward Antoine Walker, "If someone got 81 on me, I'm going to clothesline him."

Also, Bryant would need the cooperation of his teammates, and his relationship with them, particularly power forward Lamar Odom and point guard Smush Parker, remains iffy. They love his talent, hate his propensities for criticizing them and ignoring them during games. Would the other Lakers let him get 100? Scottie Pippen, who was famously the "other star" when Jordan was in his prime, watched the game on TV and said on *Cold Pizza* the following day, "[With Michael] you wanted to feed him the ball. You wanted to see him succeed.... You look at a player like Lamar Odom.... He didn't really step up in the game last night. He didn't seem like he wanted to play a role."

And would Jackson let Bryant get 100? Their relationship was volatile, to say the least, before this season, but it's better now—Kobe's talent and toughness have earned Jackson's respect. On Monday, Jackson was asked if he could envision a 100-point scenario. "Well, I don't think anyone, in this era, could imagine that," he said. "Then again, I couldn't have imagined 81 either."

Neither could Bryant. "To sit here and say I grasp what happened would be lying," he said on Sunday. "Not even in my dreams." But now that he has 81, you can bank this: some of Kobe's dreams have three digits.

Bryant hits a game winning shot at the buzzer in overtime to beat the Suns.

Bryant shoots a runner in the lane against Philadelphia. The Lakers finished the 2005–06 regular season at 45–37.

BRYANT
8
SIXERS
IGUODALA
9
4

Excerpted from SPORTS ILLUSTRATED, April 17, 2006

The Great Unknown

Ten seasons into a certain Hall of Fame career, Kobe Bryant remains, to teammates and opponents, admirers and haters, as big a mystery as ever

BY JACK McCALLUM and L. JON WERTHEIM

I. THE IMAGE

"Some people are going to like me, some people aren't going to like me," Kobe Bryant is saying after a practice at the Lakers' El Segundo training facility in late March. "The people who don't, just have to understand who I truly am, and that can only happen through time. That's why you don't see me doing talk shows and things like that."

Opponents who marveled at Bryant's ability to compartmentalize his life while facing charges for felony sexual assault of an employee at a luxury hotel in Eagle, Colo., in 2003—he would fly to Eagle in the morning for proceedings in the case, then play an outstanding game in Los Angeles that night—say he has become an even more steely-eyed assassin since his legal difficulties. "It's like he's paying everybody back," says Portland Trail Blazers guard Sebastian Telfair. "It's like he's thinking, The best way for me to get my image back is to go out there and kill everybody. He wants to, like, murder you."

Were you expecting a chastened, contrite post-Eagle Kobe? Bryant is adamant in his assertion that there is not—and never will be—a charm campaign to mend his image. The Lakers didn't do anything official to try to restore Bryant as an icon to the denizens of Staples Center, no meet-and-greets with season-ticket holders, no orchestrated interviews with Oprah or Ed Bradley. "Kobe's approach was: Let's have it be real, professional on and off the court; handle yourself the right way, every day," says John Black, the Lakers' director of public relations. "And, over time, people will respect that."

Bryant waits for the opening tip against the Clippers in 2005.

NBA commissioner David Stern recalls the pleas for Bryant to be suspended even after the sexual assault charges against him were dropped. "That is not the American way," says Stern, who adds that "it's clear that Kobe hasn't made this into a case of either rehabilitation or image management. It's Kobe being Kobe."

Even before Eagle, Bryant's image was that of a loner, a fierce individualist who didn't connect with his teammates or the public at large. Though several people close to him bemoan his lack of a common touch, Bryant disputes his portrayal. "I never was as lonely and solitary as people thought," he says. "When I first came [into the NBA] I didn't know much about anything. So I kind of sheltered myself off. But I was 17 when I got here. Seventeen! It was hard figuring out who I was."

Bryant's claims to the contrary, there are signs that he cares about refurbishing his image, at least in select forums. Earlier this year he wrote a first person article for *Dime*, the hoops fanzine, addressing a wide range of issues. Most revealing were his observations about his relationship with the Black community. "I never felt like I deserved to be part of our tradition because I grew up overseas, in Italy," he wrote. "…I never truly believed that my own people wanted to identify with me."

As the editors wrote in an explanatory note in the front of the magazine, "This story was important to Kobe; he viewed it as an opportunity to communicate unfiltered and uncensored with the public."

The article, of course, was a no-risk proposition, Bryant calling the shots, leaving little—potentially unpleasant lines of inquiry, follow-up questions, unflattering photos—to the control of others. There was no mention of the Colorado incident nor his role in splintering the Lakers and their run at a dynasty.

II. THE PLAYER

For all the contradictions swirling about him, there is this unassailable truth: Bryant is the game's best all-around player. And according to many, including Trail Blazers coach Nate McMillan, he's getting better. "If you want to find a player to build around, he's probably it," says McMillan. "He's got great size for a guard, he's pretty impossible to defend, and he is hard to score against when he hunkers down on defense."

Facing the defense, Bryant has no peer. He can avoid defenders like a stunt driver swerving

> **"I wanted Kobe to move into the realm where he has a nurturing element," says Jackson. "And that's come out this year. He's patient, accepting, friendlier to teammates."**

through oncoming traffic. He can blow by for a dunk, pull up for a short jumper, or simply rise up and hit a long-range, heavily contested perimeter missile.

With his back to the defense, Bryant is equally dangerous. If a defender gives him space, he faces up and banks in a jump shot. If a defender crowds him, he speeds past or overpowers him. If he's double-teamed, he up-fakes, pivots, and squeezes between defenders for a layup, almost always without traveling. Innate athleticism aside, he has labored like a Broadway dancer to perfect his footwork.

Besides leading the league in scoring, Bryant ranked in the top 10 at week's end in steals, minutes, field goals attempted, field goals made, three-pointers attempted, three-pointers made, free throws attempted, free throws made, and player efficiency rating.

It's been three decades since a player from a .500-level team was the league's MVP—that was Kareem Abdul-Jabbar, who took the 1975–76 award even though his Lakers finished 40–42. With Bryant's Lakers 41–37 and tied for seventh place in the Western Conference through Sunday, even the "M-V-P!" cheers that erupt from time to time in Staples Center are tepid. But his play has been so outstanding this season that he must be on any short list of candidates.

"I'm not saying that he's the most valuable player, but he's certainly the best player," says Phoenix Suns coach Mike D'Antoni. "And it's not even close. He is utterly dominant."

III. THE GHOST

At times Bryant almost eerily channels Michael Jordan on the court—the same fade-away jumper, the same feral, crouched-panther stance on defense, the same pigeon-toed walk downcourt. But the debate over whether Kobe is the next Jordan is settled. As much as Madison Avenue might have wanted Bryant's cross-over appeal to be as impressive as his crossover dribble, it is not. Jordan's default facial expression was a wide smile, Bryant's a cloudy frown. Still, the specter of Jordan looms inescapably over Bryant.

Like Jordan, he is capable of reducing even All-Stars to little kids in his presence. In a nearly deserted hallway long after a late-March game against Sacramento, Bryant emerged from the locker room to find his wife, Vanessa, and three-year-old daughter, Natalia, waiting for him. Kings forward Ron Artest, whom Bryant had badly outplayed on this evening, came by, carrying a throwaway camera and his five-year-old son, Ron Ron. "Kobe, would you take a picture with my boy?" Artest asked, the way a timid kid would ask a teacher for a favor. "Sure," said Kobe, stationing himself between Natalia and Ron Ron as Artest snapped away.

While Jordan, too,could be forbidding to other players, he also projected warmth—far more than Bryant does. "When players sit around, Kobe's not a guy you might talk about and say, 'He's such a good dude,' like a Kevin Garnett," says Los Angeles Clippers guard Cuttino Mobley. "Nobody knows Kobe that well. He's not a sociable guy. That's not a fault; it's just his preference. When I was a rookie [in Houston], Scottie Pippen told me that Michael would go out with his teammates sometimes. He included guys and balanced everything out. I'm not sure Kobe does that."

"From a talent standpoint, he may be better than Jordan was at this stage of his career," says Clippers coach Mike Dunleavy. "The part of his game that he has to get better as opposed to Jordan is in the leadership department, how players respond to him, how he gets along, creating a chemistry. Players loved playing with Jordan. I don't know whether they do with Kobe."

It should be noted that Jordan's ubercompetitiveness, which sometimes led him to humiliate his teammates, was generally seen as a positive, perhaps because he did it (mostly) behind closed doors, partly because he was, well,

Michael. The same trait in Bryant is often seen as objectionable. "When he's being the nice Kobe, he's good with everybody," says San Antonio Spurs forward Robert Horry, a teammate of Bryant's in L.A. for seven seasons. "But when he's being the butthole Kobe, he's difficult. There were days when the second team would beat the first team, and he wouldn't speak to guys because he wanted to get back onto the court and beat them. He's just very passionate about his basketball."

As dominant as Jordan was, he had a way of refraining from lording it over his opponents. He disagreed, of course, with suggestions that there were actually defenders who could stop him (such as Detroit's Joe Dumars or Cleveland's Craig Ehlo), but he usually did it with grace and good humor.

Bryant does not. After he dropped 51 points on Raja Bell in a loss to the Suns last Friday, he was asked about the physical battle Bell had given him. Bryant shot the questioner a look that said, Are you nuts? "Raja Bell?" he said, enunciating the name as if it were a contagious disease. "I don't even think about him. Man, I got bigger fish to fry than Raja Bell."

In *The Last Season*, Phil Jackson's tell-almost-all book about the 2003–04 season, the Lakers' coach labeled Bryant "uncoachable" and admitted that he tried to persuade general manager Mitch Kupchak to unload him before the February trading deadline. "[Kobe] could have been heir apparent to MJ and maybe won as many championships," Jackson wrote. "He may still win a championship or two, but the boyish hero image has been replaced by that of a callous gun for hire."

Two years later, having returned to the Los Angeles bench, Jackson is predictably conciliatory, insisting that Bryant would, for example, no longer defiantly remove himself from the offense, as he did during an infamous one-shot first half against the Kings late in the 2003–04 season. "Kobe now plays that role of involving guys in the offense without taking himself out," says Jackson. "It used to be an either-or situation, black or white.

"I wanted Kobe to move into the realm where he's not only the driving force by his play but also has a nurturing element," the Lakers' coach adds. "And that is what has come out this year. He's patient, accepting, and friendlier to his teammates."

Some of the Lakers agree. "Before, Kobe wouldn't really say much and would just lead by playing hard, coming early, and staying late," says forward Devean George, who among his current teammates has been with Bryant the longest (seven years). "Now he's more vocal. Some of the younger guys, it might bother them. They're still trying to find their way. Kobe being the superstar player and a big name, it holds weight when he yells. But he likes everybody on the team. I don't think he's doing it to put anyone down."

Bryant's most important relationship among his teammates is with talented 6'10" forward Lamar Odom. Bryant and Odom have the potential to be a 21st-century version of Jordan and Pippen. But Odom sometimes defers to Bryant too much; around the league it is generally thought that the Lakers' chances of flourishing in the postseason depend on how much Odom asserts himself.

One of the most intriguing subplots of the Lakers' season involves whether Bryant and Odom nearly came to blows after a 94–91 loss to the Wizards in Washington on Dec. 26. With five seconds remaining, Bryant turned the ball over but pinned the blame on Odom for a botched pick-and-roll. The principals say there was no subsequent altercation; other teammates confirm that harsh words were exchanged. Nevertheless, Odom, who has heard throughout his career how much better he would be if he had a warrior's mentality, sometimes seems in awe of Bryant's single-minded dedication to winning. "Kobe goes after it as hard as anybody in the league," says Odom. "He wants to win. That's what you have to understand about him."

Still, it's hard to determine where the party line stops and reality begins. His teammates know that they will face Bryant's wrath if they don't get him the ball in clutch situations…and may face it anyway. After the Lakers lost close games at New Jersey (92–89 on March 17) and Cleveland (96–95 two days later), Bryant pointed fingers.

Against the Nets, Odom had trouble inbounding the ball and neglected to call timeout with 13 seconds remaining. That, Bryant said afterward, led to a broken play and an awkward Bryant miss as time expired. Bryant also brought Luke Walton into that conversation, angrily pointing to a spot on the floor where he presumably thought the Lakers' forward should've been.

In the loss to the Cavaliers, it was Walton who had a hard time getting the ball inbounds to Bryant on a last-shot play. Eventually he did, but Bryant received the pass 35 feet from the basket and missed a shot as time expired. After the game Bryant said that Walton should've called a timeout. "I guess I could have called a timeout," responded an uncharacteristically piqued Walton, "but it's a 48-minute game and we didn't lose because I didn't call a timeout."

IV. THE BELIEVERS

Bryant and his family have, at least publicly, lived down the embarrassment of Eagle. "My wife and daughter are my refuge," Kobe claims. The Bryants are expecting their second daughter in May. "Natalia can't wait to be a big sister," says Bryant. And that is all he'll say on the subject.

Off the court Bryant certainly has his supporters. Earlier this year Bryant paid a visit to his high school alma mater, Lower Merion in suburban Philadelphia, where he was approached by a member of the girls' basketball team. "How come you don't hook us up with shoes?" she asked.

The following day the girls' team received $17,000 worth of Nike shoes and gear. Last month, as the Lower Merion boys' team rode on a bus to the state championship game, Bryant called the team's captains to offer encouragement. He also left a message on the voicemail of coach Gregg Downer offering words of advice: "The key for the kids to understand is: refuse to lose. Period. It's one game. Win this game. Worry about the next when it comes.… I'm sure you've had 'em working hard all season long. This is their moment to take. Just make sure they go out there and do it. Call me after you kick their asses. All right, brother. Out."

Bryant on the court against the Spurs in 2006.

"Look, I know half the people out there think he's nasty or he's selfish," says Downer. "But I'm telling you, there's a lot of good in his heart."

Duke's Mike Krzyzewski, who has built his success on athletes with virtuous reputations, has asked Bryant to be the leader of the 2008 Olympic team in Beijing. "It's Kobe's time,"

Coach K says of Bryant. "He's 27 years old. He should try to assume a position of leadership [on] the team. I would think he's very hungry to do this. I see him fitting in very, very well."

Stern echoes that sentiment. "I have no qualms whatsoever about Kobe carrying the Olympic standard for us," the commissioner says. "In fact, I think it's great."

Nike had signed Bryant to a five-year, $45 million deal just days before the Colorado charges. According to Ralph Greene, the company's director for global basketball, Nike never came close to severing ties with Bryant. "He never ceased to be an intriguing basketball player or someone who could help us," says Greene. "And we knew we could help him."

Still, Nike did more or less hide Bryant for almost three years, launching their first Kobe shoe, the Zoom Kobe I, only this February. The decision to come out with a Bryant model, Greene says, was not motivated by market research or focus group testing. "In terms of Kobe's endorsement value, we always knew that his play on the court was going to be the motivating factor."

V. THE HATERS

For an athlete to refurbish his image, he needs to advance through a set of concentric circles—the home fan, the basketball fan, the nonfan. Even after Eagle, Bryant remained in the good graces of most Lakers acolytes, particularly the Hollywood crowd, which was always more enthralled with Bryant's graceful acrobatics than with Shaquille O'Neal's brute force. Staples became, in effect, Bryant's personal decontamination chamber. This season, mostly by dint of his play, Bryant is winning back basketball fans outside of L.A. In 2006 he was the second-leading All-Star vote getter, behind only Yao Ming, who is always buoyed by an international voting bloc.

Yet even within the game, there is a reluctance to fully embrace Bryant's virtuosity. His 81-point game against the Toronto Raptors at Staples Center on Jan. 22 drew, at best, ambivalent reviews. Sniffed Miami Heat coach Pat Riley, "It's remarkable, the execution and the efficiency, but we've got a lot of guys in this league, if they took 70 shots, they'd score a lot of points." (For the record, Bryant took only 46 shots.)

Here's a laugh: New Jersey's Vince Carter expressed concern for the underlying message sent by the four-score-and-one. "The only bad thing about it is, young kids, whose minds are easily warped, are going to think, Ohhh, I am going to go out there and do it instead of [putting] the team concept first." This is the same Vince Carter who once wore his iPod through a layup line, all but extorted a trade from Toronto to New Jersey, and loves to hoist fallaway 30-footers.

More damning, among the general public, Bryant's Q rating—which measures a celebrity's recognition and likability—remains subterranean. In an extensive poll regarding 1,750 celebrities conducted last month, Bryant achieved a positive Q-rating score of 12 and a negative score of 47. The average score was 17/25.Omarosa Manigault-Stallworth, the conniving *Apprentice* contestant, ranked dead last, scoring 3/82. Bryant was in the company of Vince McMahon, Robert Blake, and even Barry Bonds.

"Kobe is easily in the bottom fifth," says Steven Levitt, president of Marketing Evaluations, the Long Island–based company that measures Q ratings. "It's not enough to have a great game or lead the league in scoring to overcome the disgrace that's been heaped upon him. His negative is four times his positive. That should scare the hell out of [any potential sponsor]. You won't sell batteries or peanut butter or Ball Park hot dogs or even Gatorade with that ranking."

In 2002 Reebok executive Henry (Que) Gaskins, then Philadelphia 76ers guard Allen Iverson's adviser, memorably suggested that Bryant's skills

"It's like he's thinking, The best way to get my image back is to go out and kill everybody." says Telfair. "He wants to, like, murder you."

outpaced his marketability to shoe companies because he didn't have any street cred.

Todd Boyd, a professor at USC's School of Cinema-Television and author of *Young, Black, Rich, and Famous: The Rise of the NBA, the Hip Hop Invasion, and the Transformation of American Culture*, is more harsh. "Saying Kobe has street cred is like saying Dick Cheney has street cred." Boyd says that Bryant's image problems in part stem from an ambiguous racial identity. "If Kobe had been a white American player, people would have seen him as someone visibly different from the NBA population and accepted him as an individual who didn't fit the culture. Well, he's African American, but as far as his class and disposition, he's not what people normally associate with NBA players. Then he gets charged with this crime, and suddenly [he seems] like everybody else.... I honestly can't name any African Americans not professing to be Lakers fans who like Kobe."

VI. THE LAST SHOT

Bryant would dispute Boyd's contention. It is imperative to remember how he grew up, as a loner in Italy, the relatively privileged son of a former NBA player turned expatriate. Kobe's first hoops hero was not Michael Jordan or Julius Erving but D'Antoni, a heady white point guard from West Virginia who was Italy's most famous professional player during Kobe's formative years. Bryant adopted jersey number 8 because that was D'Antoni's number.

There are other Black athletes who grew up in privileged circumstances, of course, but rarely was one as divorced from the African American experience as Bryant was. Outside Phoenix's America West Arena, after his 51-point performance last Friday, he referred to his first-person essay in *Dime*, in which he wrote, "When I went to visit the victims of Hurricane Katrina and saw how their faces lit up when they saw me, how they embraced me and how my presence lifted their spirits, I realized how wrong I'd been about everything. I'd wasted all these years wanting to do things for our people, but thinking I wasn't the one to do them, that I wouldn't be welcomed. But now I see that isn't true. The experience of Katrina and my own personal struggles brought me closer to our people." He is ready, he says, to wear the mantle of African American hero.

But Bryant seems to want to get only so close to the larger public, to not even reveal that he cares about it. Here's more Kobe, after that March practice at the Lakers' training facility: "You can have one person say, 'He's got a terrible image.' And you can have another person say, 'He has a great image.' What do people think of me? It's all over the place. That doesn't really give you much, does it?"

SPALDING

Bryant scores past LeBron James, during the King's first reign in Cleveland, in 2007.

Bryant battles Boston's Ray Allen for a rebound in 2007.

LAKERS
24

Bryant slams one home as the Celtics can only watch in 2007.

LOS ANGELES LAKERS
A.com
LAKERS
24
THE BICYCLE CASINO
DIRECTV
WACHOVIA
Sempra Energy
PEPSI
Miller Lite
GREAT TASTE...

Excerpted from Sports Illustrated, June 2, 2008

Kobe's Killer Instinct

Nobody wants to win as much as Kobe Bryant because nobody *needs* to win as much as he does. From childhood to the Western finals, the Lakers star has been obsessed with dominating the court

BY CHRIS BALLARD

A great moment in humility it was not. After scoring 25 of his 27 points in the second half of Game 1 of the Western Conference finals last week against the San Antonio Spurs, Los Angeles Lakers star Kobe Bryant said of his strong finishing kick, "I can get off"—that is, score at will—"at any time. In the second half I did that."

Granted, Bryant was just being honest, but tact would dictate that he let others say such things about him. As you may have noticed, though, Bryant isn't big on tact. Time and again over the last decade he has announced the particulars of his awesomeness. As teammate Luke Walton dryly puts it, "Kobe does not lack for confidence."

Just as Bryant's bravado irks some—O.K., many—it also makes him riveting to watch when he does get off: like the man himself, the manner in which he bears down is never subtle. Spurs forward Bruce Bowen, Bryant's foil these many years, says there's no indicator of an impending scoring binge, joking that you can't tell "by the way he chews his gum or something." But that's not true at all. Rather, his eruptions are almost comically predictable. Former teammate Devean George, now with the Dallas Mavericks, speaks of "that Kobe face where he starts looking around all pissed off." His coach at Lower Merion High in Ardmore, Pa., Gregg Downer, says he can recognize this expression even on TV. In these moments Bryant's youthful impudence, which flummoxed Del Harris when he was L.A.'s coach during Bryant's first two years in the league, resurfaces. "Kobe would put it on the floor and start going between his legs, back and forth, back and forth," says Harris, "and only then would he decide what to do."

So there was Kobe on May 21, with the Lakers down 20 in the third quarter and the

Celebrating a victory against Denver in the playoffs in 2008.

L.A. crowd starting to boo, whipping the ball between his legs and shaking his noggin at Bowen like some enormous, ticked-off bobblehead. What followed seemed, in retrospect, inevitable: the deep jumpers, the twisting drives, the scowls, and, finally, a cold-blooded Bryant pull-up in the lane with 23.9 seconds left to cap the 89–85 comeback win. Watching him manhandle the game, you could feel the series tilting westward, and indeed the Lakers were up two games to one after a 101–71 blowout last Friday and a 103–84 loss in Game 3 on Sunday.

Call it what you will: killer instinct, competitive fire, hatred of losing, or, as Boston Celtics reserve guard Sam Cassell once said, "that Jordan thing." It's what has spurred Bryant all these years, what the Lakers will rely on if they are to win their first post-Shaq championship, what separates Kobe from the rest of the NBA. In 2002 Bryant said, "There's only two real killers in this league," meaning himself and Michael Jordan. Well, now there is only one. And it ain't Fabricio Oberto.

Because Kobe is Kobe, however, he cannot (or will not) soften his edge, the way Jordan did with his buddy-buddy NBA friendships, his who-would-have-thunk smirk or his endorsa-riffic smile. With Bryant, it manifests itself during practice, during games, during summer workouts, during conversation. Even in his dreams he is probably swatting a Connie Hawkins finger roll into the third row. "He can't turn it off, even if he tried," says George, one of a handful of NBA players relatively close to Bryant. And for that Kobe has often been pilloried. But is this really fair? "Kobe wants it so badly that he rubs an awful lot of people the wrong way," says Lakers consultant Tex Winter, the guru of the triangle offense, who has known Bryant since 1999. "But they're not willing to understand what's inside the guy."

O.K., then, let's try to understand. Starting at the beginning, moment by basketball moment.

It's 1989, and Bryant is 11 years old and living in Italy, where his father, Joe, is playing professional basketball. One day Kobe bugs Brian Shaw, a Boston Celtics first-round pick playing in Rome because of a contract dispute, to go one-on-one. Eventually Shaw agrees to a game of H-O-R-S-E. "To this day Kobe claims he beat me," says Shaw, now a Lakers assistant. "I'm like, Right, [I'm really trying to beat] an 11-year-old kid. But he's serious." Even back then Shaw noticed something different. "His dad was a good player, but he was the opposite of Kobe, real laid-back," says Shaw. "Kobe was out there challenging grown men to play one-on-one, and he really thought he could win."

It's early 1992, and Bryant is an eighth-grader in the suburbs of Philadelphia, skinny as an unfurled paper clip. He is playing against the Lower Merion varsity in an informal scrimmage. The older teens are taken aback. "Here's this kid, and he has no fear of us at all," says Doug Young, then a sophomore. "He's throwing elbows, setting hard screens." Bryant was not the best player on the floor that day—not yet—but he was close.

It's 1995, and Bryant is the senior leader of the Lower Merion team, obsessed with winning a state championship. He comes to the gym at 5 a.m. to work out before school, stays until 7 p.m. afterward. It's all part of the plan. When the Aces lost in the playoffs the previous spring, Bryant stood in the locker room, interrupting the seniors as they hugged each other, and all but guaranteed a title, adding, "The work starts now." (Bryant remains so amped about his alma mater that when he taped a video message for the team a few years ago, it contained few of the usual platitudes and instead had Bryant reeling off a bunch of expletives and exhorting the boys to "take care of f— business!")

During the Kobe era at Lower Merion no moment was inconsequential, no drill unworthy of ultimate concentration. In one practice during his senior year, "just a random Tuesday," as Coach Downer recalls, Bryant was engaged

Because Kobe is Kobe, however, he cannot (or will not) soften his edge, the way Jordan did with his buddy-buddy NBA friendships, his who-would-have-thunk smirk or his endorsa-riffic smile.

in a three-on-three drill in a game to 10. One of his teammates was Rob Schwartz, a 5'7" junior benchwarmer. With the game tied at nine, Schwartz had an opening, drove to the basket, and missed, allowing the other side to score and win. "Now, most kids go to the water fountain and move on," says Downer. Not Bryant. He chased Schwartz into the hallway and berated him. It didn't stop there, either. "Ever get the feeling someone is staring at you—you don't have to look at them, but you know it?" says Schwartz. "I felt his eyes on me for the next 20 minutes. It was like, by losing that drill, I'd lost us the state championship."

Bryant had already begun to coax teammates into staying late or coming in at odd hours so he could hone his skills. "We'd play games of one-on-one to 100," says Schwartz. "Sometimes he'd score 80 points before I got one basket. I think the best I ever did was to lose 100–12." Imagine the focus required to score 80 freakin' baskets before your opponent scores one. And Bryant's probably still pissed that Schwartz broke double digits.

It's 1996, and the Lakers call in Bryant, fresh off his senior prom—he took pop singer Brandy, you might recall—for a predraft workout at the Inglewood High gym. In attendance are GM Jerry West and two members of L.A.'s media relations staff, John Black and Raymond Ridder. Bryant is to play one-on-one against Michael Cooper, the former Lakers guard and one of the premier defenders in NBA history. Cooper is 40 years old but still in great shape, wiry and long and stronger than the teenaged Bryant. The game is not even close. "It was like Cooper was mesmerized by him," says Ridder, now the Golden State Warriors' executive director of media relations. After 10 minutes West stands up. "That's it, I've seen enough," Ridder remembers West saying. "He's better than anyone we've got on the team right now. Let's go."

It would be a pattern: Bryant bearing down on players he once idolized. At Magic Johnson's summer charity game in 1998 he went after Orlando Magic star Penny Hardaway so hard—in a charity game—that Hardaway spent the fall telling people he couldn't wait to play the Lakers so he could go back at Bryant. And, more famously, Kobe attempted to go one-on-one against Jordan in the '98 All-Star Game, waving off a screen from Karl Malone. Take your pick-and-rolling butt out of here; I've got Jordan iso'd! That one didn't go over so well with the Mailman. "When young guys tell me to get out of the way," Malone said at the time, "that's a game I don't need to be in."

In Bryant's mind, however, no one is unbeatable. As a rookie with the Lakers, despite his coming straight out of high school, he approached Harris. "He said, 'Coach, if you just give me the ball and clear out, I can beat anybody in this league,'" recalls Harris. When that pitch didn't work, the 6'6" Bryant returned. "Then he'd say, 'Coach, I can post up anybody who's guarding me. If you just get me in there and clear it out, I can post up anybody.'" Harris chuckles. "I said, 'Kobe, I know you can, but right now you can't do it at a high enough rate for the team we have, and I'm not going to tell Shaquille O'Neal to get out of the way so you can do this.' Kobe didn't like it. He understood it, but in his heart he didn't accept it."

It is 2000, and Bryant is an All-Star and franchise player. Still, after guard Isaiah Rider signs as a free agent, Bryant repeatedly forces him to play one-on-one after practice—Bryant wins, of course—to reinforce his alpha–alpha male status. When six-time All-Star guard Mitch Richmond arrives the next year, he gets the same. "He was the man, and he wanted us to know it," says Richmond. "He was never mean or personal about it, it's just how he was."

Not that Bryant never loses, but beat him at your own risk. Decline a rematch and...well, that's not an option. "If you scored on him in practice or did something to embarrass him, he would just keep on challenging you and challenging you until you stayed after and played him so he could put his will on you and dominate you," says Shaw, Bryant's teammate from 1999 to 2003. This included not allowing players to leave the court. Literally. "He'd stand in our way and say, 'Nah, nah, we're gonna play. I want you to do that [move] again,'" Shaw says. "And you might be tired and say, 'Nah, I did it in practice.' But he was just relentless and persistent until finally you'd go play, and he'd go at you."

And just as he once did with Rob Schwartz, Bryant keeps NBA teammates after practice as guinea pigs. He unveils a spin move or a crossover or something else he has picked up watching tape and does it over and over and over. "The crazy thing about it is, he has the ability to put new elements in his game overnight," says George, a Laker from 1999 to 2006 and a frequent target of Kobe's requests. "He might say, 'Stay after and guard this move. Let me try it on you,' and he'll do it the next day in the game." George pauses to let this sink in. "Most of us, we'll try it alone, then we'll try it in practice, then in a scrimmage, and only then will we bring it out for a game. He'd do it the next day—and it would work."

It's 2003, and Bryant is getting worked up in an interview while talking about a variation on a move: a jab step-and-pause, where you sink deep, hesitate to let the defender relax, and, instead of bringing the jab foot back, push off it. Soon enough, Bryant is out of his chair and using the reporter as a defender on the carpeted floor. Then he has the reporter trying the move. Some people are Star Wars nerds; Bryant is a basketball nerd. "I think Kobe's actually a little bit embarrassed by his love of basketball," says Downer. "People called him a loner, but it's just that basketball is all he wants to focus on. I think he's part of a dying breed that loves the game that way."

That's why Bryant gets so excited to meet kindred souls. Asked last week about Spurs coach Gregg Popovich, Bryant's face lit up as he remembered the time he played for Pop. "I was really hoping he'd run us through one of those rigorous practices he does," said Bryant, who got his wish. By the way, Kobe was talking about practice for the '05 All-Star Game.

Now it's 2008, the Western Conference finals. Bryant is finally where he wants to be: an MVP playing on his team, no behemoth Hall of Famer to get in the way of post-ups, within reach of a title. He is also, by almost all accounts, the best player in the league. "It's not even close," says one Western Conference scout. "The difference between him and LeBron [James] is like [the one between] a Maserati and a Volvo."

The scout has other things to say about Bryant. For example, on his weaknesses: "Um, let me think...[long pause]...No, I don't think he has any." On his athleticism: "There are probably 10 [with more] in the league"—he names Andre Iguodala, Josh Smith, Dwight Howard, and J.R. Smith as examples—"but no one uses his as well as Kobe. Just watch his footwork sometime." And on his focus: "There's a difference between loving basketball and liking basketball. There are only about 30 guys in the league who love it, who play year-round. Allen Iverson loves to play when the lights come on. Kobe loves doing the s— before the lights come on."

This thing, this freakish compulsion, may be the hardest element of the game to quantify. There are no plus-minus stats to measure a player's ruthlessness, his desire to beat his opponent so badly he'll need therapy to recover. One thing's for sure: you can't teach it. If so, Eddy Curry would be All-NBA and Derrick Coleman would be getting ready for his induction ceremony in Springfield, Mass. But people know it when they see it. GMs, coaches, and scouts cite only a few others who have a similar drive—Tim Duncan, Kevin Garnett, Manu Ginóbili, Steve Nash, Chris Paul, and Deron Williams—though they make clear that none of those stars are in Kobe's league. (In an SI poll earlier this season Bryant was a runaway winner as the opponent players feared most, at 35%.)

Even some of the great ones lacked it. Kareem Abdul-Jabbar says that when he was young, rather than challenging everyone as Kobe does, he "just wanted peace." "I think it's a quirk of personality," says Abdul-Jabbar. "Some of us are like Napoleon, and some are Walter Mitty."

Idan Ravin, a personal trainer who works with Paul, Carmelo Anthony, Gilbert Arenas, and Elton Brand and is known by some in the league as "the hoops whisperer" for his effect on players, has even broken killer instinct down into components: love of the game, ambition, obsessive-compulsive behavior, arrogance/confidence, selfishness, and nonculpability/guiltlessness. He sees them all in Bryant.

"If he's a ruthless s.o.b., I kind of respect that," says Ravin. "Why should he be passing up opportunities? Why pass it to a guy who doesn't work as hard, who doesn't want it like you do?"

Even now, every little challenge matters to Bryant. Here he is at the end of a practice last week. Each Laker has to take a free throw. Everybody hits his except Bryant, who rims one out. The only shooter left is Derek Fisher, who shot 88.3% from the line this season. Bryant stands to the side of the basket, fidgeting. As Fisher's shot arcs toward the rim, Bryant suddenly takes two quick steps and leaps to goaltend the attempt. "Of course," forward Lamar Odom says later, "he couldn't be the only one to miss."

So, you see, this is Kobe, all of this. Sometimes childish, sometimes regal, sometimes stubborn, always relentless. This is a guy who, according to Nike spokesperson KeJuan Wilkins, had the company shave a couple of millimeters off the bottom of his signature shoe because "in his mind that gave him a hundredth of a second better reaction time." A guy who has played the last three months with a torn ligament in the pinkie of his shooting hand. A guy who, says teammate Coby Karl, considers himself "an expert at fouling without getting called for it." (Watch how Bryant uses the back of his hand, not the front, to push off on defenders and a closed-fist forearm to exert leverage.) A guy who says of being guarded by the physical Bowen, "It'll be fun"—and actually means it. A guy who, no matter what he does, will never get the chance to play the one game he'd die for: Bryant versus Jordan, each in his prime. "There'd be blood on the floor by the end," says Winter, who has coached them both.

This is Kobe Bryant, age 29, in pursuit of his fourth NBA title. Even if it's hard for us to understand him, perhaps it's time that we appreciate him. •

at&t
at&t
THERE CAN ONLY BE ONE

Bryant stands below the video board at TD Garden during the NBA Finals in 2008. The Lakers lost to the Celtics in six games.

NIKE
NIKE
USA

Bryant, LeBron James, Dwyane Wade, and Carmelo Anthony celebrate winning the gold medal against Spain at the Beijing Olympics in 2008. Kobe also helped Team USA take home the gold in 2012 in London.

Bryant shoots over Denver's Carmelo Anthony during the playoffs in 2009.

ANTHONY
15
BILLUPS
7
DENVER
1

Excerpted from SPORTS ILLUSTRATED, June 22, 2009

Satisfaction

The Lakers are NBA champions again, and it's because they have a star who would settle for nothing less

BY CHRIS BALLARD

It is 2 a.m. on Thursday during the second week of the NBA Finals, and Kobe Bryant cannot sleep. In less than 24 hours the Lakers will make an unlikely comeback to win Game 4 in overtime, and three days later after a masterly 30-point performance in Game 5, Bryant will again be a champion.

He will raise the Larry O'Brien trophy in his long arms, and he will laugh and hug his teammates long and deep and, yes, even tear up a little. The mask of intensity he has worn for months will finally fall.

But for now it remains. For now the Lakers lead the Magic 2–1 but are recovering from a painful loss in which Bryant missed late-game free throws. So he sits in a high-backed leather chair in the lobby of the Ritz-Carlton in Orlando, surrounded by chandeliers and white orchids and gleaming white floors, in the company of friends—a group including his security guy, team employees, and trainers—but alone. He says little, the hood of his sweatshirt pulled over his scalp, his eyes staring into the inky night, past the windows and the palm trees. He holds a Corona but rarely brings it to his lips. He looks like a man so tired he cannot sleep, a man nearing the end of a long journey. It is one that began well before November, when this season started, or even last June, when the Lakers fell to the Celtics in the Finals. As he will later explain in a quiet moment, he divides his career into two bodies of work: "the Shaquille era and the post-Shaquille era." Since the post-Shaq era began in 2004, when the Lakers traded O'Neal to Miami, many have doubted, again and again, that Bryant would ever earn a ring on his own. And while he has dismissed those who classify his legacy as Shaq-dependent, calling them "idiotic," he also knows how close he is to banishing that perception.

Minutes pass. Bryant stares and says nothing. He has waited this long. He can wait a little longer.

Thirteen years into an exceptional NBA career, this is finally Kobe Bryant's moment. Sure, these Finals were about Phil Jackson attaining his 10th ring as a coach (surpassing

HAPPY FATHER'S DAY

FROM REX AND BUDDY

BY TIM LAYDEN P. 46

Sports Illustrated

JUNE 22, 2009 | SI.COM

NBA CHAMPIONS

Kobe's Moment

P. 36

BY CHRIS BALLARD

Red Auerbach's record) and guard Derek Fisher's nerveless performance in Game 4 (hitting a pair of clutch three-pointers to swing the series in Los Angeles' direction) and the emergence of 23-year-old Dwight Howard (proving, as he took the Magic to the Finals, that a big man need not scowl to be dominant). But let's be honest: this has been about Kobe all along.

So what do we make of him now? As polarizing a figure as there is in the league, he is deified in L.A. and often detested elsewhere, yet not even his detractors can deny his talent or accomplishments. At 30, Bryant has four championship rings (one more than Michael Jordan at the same age), two scoring titles, an MVP award, and now a Finals MVP award. He has won for six coaches and as part of starting lineups that included Travis Knight and Smush Parker, suffering but one losing season (and when it comes to Bryant, suffering really is the right term). He has accomplished all this while playing for one team, showing the single-town loyalty fans cherish in their sports heroes. Those who would claim that he is a poor teammate or a poor leader would seem to be finally out of ammunition.

His performance in these Finals was memorable not necessarily for the bursts of scoring (though of course there were those) but for the moments that revealed both his evolution as a player and his near-desperate desire to win. The way he wrestled with Orlando's Rashard Lewis, elbowing and hooking and kneeing when he had to switch onto the 6'10" forward; the way he bared his teeth after big plays, like a feral animal; the way he dominated not only with baskets but also with passes—Bryant had nearly twice as many assists as any other player in the Finals. Though he would never admit it, his willingness to play whatever role his team needed may have reflected Bryant's awareness that the era of LeBron James and Dwight Howard is at hand, and that the best way for him to stay relevant, since he can't do it by sheer force of personality, is by winning.

So he gave himself over to this one goal as never before—which is saying a lot for Kobe. He shut down communication during the Finals, ignoring most phone calls and cutting off email. He became so ornery that his two young daughters took to calling him Grumpy, from Snow White. And he sought nothing less than a similar commitment from his teammates. When 21-year-old center Andrew Bynum came out lackluster in Game 3, Bryant lit into him during a timeout, loud enough that a sideline reporter could overhear, "Get your head in the f— game." This was not the soft, cuddly Bryant we were served up last month in ESPN's Spike Lee documentary *Kobe Doin' Work*. Rather, this was Kobe actually doing work. And it was far more compelling.

"

He dominated not only with baskets but with passes—he had nearly twice as many assists as any other player in the Finals.

Thus, to see the man as he was during these Finals, not as Nike or Lee or Bryant might prefer, is to see a portrait of him at his competitive best, a man intent on controlling his own legacy.

It's late in the first half of Game 1 at Staples Center, and Bryant is on one of those rolls. He sticks one jumper, then another. At times like these, he says, he can sense the fear in his opponent, in this case 6'6" swingman Mickael Pietrus. "They get kind of nervous and are scared to touch you," Bryant explains. "It's no fun playing against players like that." He prefers a confident opponent. "It becomes more fun for you," he says, "because it becomes a challenge."

This desire for challenges—and isn't it remarkable that in the Finals he craves added obstacles—is what Bryant has spent the last decade trying to both feed off and harness. In recent years, at Jackson's suggestion, he's turned to meditation. He's also coming to terms with the fact that it isn't that his teammates don't want to win as much he does (though this is true), it's that they don't have the capacity to want to win as much as he does. Says Gregg Downer, Bryant's coach at Lower Merion (Pa.) High and a good friend, "As difficult as Kobe can be, as demanding as he is, I think [he and his teammates] all found some middle ground, a center."

That center is this: give as much as you can, and you can play on his team. "I'm going to continue to push and push, and if my teammates can keep up, they will," Bryant says. "If they can't, then they probably won't be here."

Now it is Game 2, and Bryant is backing out of a double team, then passing to the weak side. He is trying to be a facilitator, trying to override his instincts, the ones that tell him to take over, to win this thing right here. And it's working: at the half he has the same number of shots (five) as assists.

It's a lesson he learned in the Western Conference finals against the Nuggets. Bryant was averaging 36.8 points, yet the series was tied 2–2 and L.A. was struggling, reliant on an increasingly exhausted Bryant to carry them.

Watching film, Bryant and Jackson noticed the same thing: Denver's double teams were creating avenues to the rim. The next game, Kobe made the adjustment. Doubled on the perimeter, he retreated, pulling the defense with him, then found open men who found open men. As Bynum said after that game, "When he's calm and he's moving the ball, nobody can beat us."

Bryant finished Game 5 against Denver with eight assists, then had 10 in a clinching Game 6 and was instrumental in dozens of other plays. It was, put simply, the Good Kobe. For L.A.'s coaching staff, getting Bryant to play like this has been an ongoing challenge. "He likes to make the pass for the assist of the score," says assistant Brian Shaw. "We would like him to make the pass that would lead to the pass."

Even though Bryant doesn't do this all the time, it's hard for coaches to get too upset. "There's a trust that we have because we know that he's trying to win the game," Shaw says. "There are a lot of times when Phil will call a play, but [Kobe] will have a feel for what's going on out on the floor and say, 'No, no, no. I already got something going.' Phil trusts that."

Now it is 5:30 in the morning after Game 4, and Bryant is headed to the gym. Only hours earlier the Lakers pulled out a dramatic 99–91 win to take a 3–1 series lead, and with three more chances to finish the series, the players could finally relax. There are two nights off before Game 5, and it was time to celebrate a bit, and Kobe did. For all of four hours. Now, before he goes to sleep, it is time to get in some work.

At the urging of his trainer, Tim Grover, Bryant heads to the fitness center at the Ritz-Carlton, where a couple of early-bird businessmen are shocked to share their treadmill time with an 11-time All-Star. For an hour and a half Grover takes Bryant through a series of exercises: weights, stretching, muscle-activation routines. Grover's logic is that if Bryant gets his

Bryant shoots in Game 1 of the NBA Finals in 2009 against Orlando. He was named the Finals MVP after the Lakers won the series in five games.

work in now, he can have a block of uninterrupted sleep and not disturb his rest pattern.

Bryant's work ethic is renowned, but this season he became even more obsessive. Unhappy with his physical stamina during the Finals a year ago, he asked Grover, with whom he'd worked during the off-season, to become, in essence, his personal trainer: travel with him, monitor his workouts. For Grover, who runs his business out of Chicago, and whose clients include Dwyane Wade (and, for many years, Michael Jordan), it was asking a lot. "There are only about three guys in the league I would have even considered doing this for," says Grover. "With Kobe, I knew he'd take it very seriously."

Grover's modifications were small but important. Bryant had never been an advocate of cold tubs; Grover had him taking ice baths frequently for muscle recovery. He focused on strengthening Bryant's ankles, wrists, hips—"areas that don't make you look better in your jersey but can become nagging injuries," Grover says. The result is that, despite having played for nearly three years straight due to his Olympic commitments, Bryant came into these Finals free of ankle braces, shoulder wraps, and sleeves—although his right ring finger, dislocated earlier in the season, remained taped. He even wore low-top shoes. (Bryant believes they give him a greater range of motion, and Grover concurs.) When Bryant missed those free throws in Game 3, finishing 5-of-10 from the line, Grover had him show up early the next day and spend 40 minutes just shooting foul shots. "The superstars aren't superstars just by accident," says Grover. "Michael was Michael because of what he did on and off the court; it didn't just happen. Same with Kobe. It's because of the time and effort and the knowledge that he gains and his willingness to listen to people."

It is an interesting concept, that a man long criticized for not listening to people is succeeding now because he does.

Now it is before Game 5, and it seems as if every camera in Amway Arena is trained on Bryant. His eyes are hooded, his jaw is set. This is what he came for. When Bynum says of Bryant, "Only he knows what motivates him," well, that's not really true at all. Don't we all know what motivates Bryant? As Fisher says, "He wants to be the best player to have ever played this game. That's what he works at every day."

While it is often easy to question Bryant's sincerity, it is hard to do so when the subject is his drive. "I push and push and push—that's the only way I know," Bryant says. A day earlier I had asked him about the future, when he's in his mid-30s, and whether he could ever see himself being a third option on a team. "Third option?" he said, and then he paused. He frowned slightly, rolling the idea around in his head, entertaining an existence where he orbits others, not the other way around. He wrinkled his nose at the thought, then finally answered. "I don't know; that's tough to see," he said. "One thing I've always been great at is scoring the ball. Even when I'm 35, I think I'll be a bad mother—." And with this, Bryant laughed. It must feel good to tell the truth.

Finally, the moment—his moment—is here. There is 1:12 left in Game 5, and the Lakers have both the ball and a 95–84 lead. Once again, Bryant has been superb. He has hit big shots, including an acrobatic runner across the lane, coming right to left, switching hands in midair, eluding the 6'11" Howard's reach and then hitting a soft banker before crashing onto his back; it called to mind Jordan's iconic levitating, right-to-left midair layup against the Lakers in the 1991 Finals. Again, however, it was the rest of Kobe's game that stood out. He had two steals, four blocks, six rebounds, five assists, and untold hockey assists—the passes that lead to the passes that lead to the scores that make Brian Shaw so happy.

Now, during this final Lakers timeout, Bryant heads back to the bench. He tries to lean back in his chair but cannot sit still. He attempts to control his breathing, which is quick and shallow. He bites his nails, shifts his eyes; he looks nervous, like a teenager about to ask a girl out on a first date. Then, finally, shyly, he smiles. It is a genuine smile, oddly naked. It is a Bryant we rarely see.

Soon, he will accept the MVP trophy and bring Natalia, 6, and Gianna, 3, onstage. Then he will run back to the locker room, slithering through the hallway crowd, shouting, "Oh! My! God!" and he will make sure to drench Jackson in champagne, and then he will sit before the media at a podium and grin goofily and talk about getting "a big old monkey off my back" and rest his cheeks in between his hands and say how it feels as if he's dreaming and how he "can't believe this moment is here." And then he will head to the Ritz to celebrate, still wearing his champagne-soaked T-shirt and shorts, a cigar protruding from his mouth, punch-drunk and pleased to take photos with all comers, no longer the child prodigy, no longer the petulant sidekick, no longer the selfish ball hog, no longer the Michael Jordan wannabe, but just Kobe Bryant, champion.

Bryant celebrates winning his fourth championship—and his first without Shaquille O'Neal— in 2009 with his wife, Vanessa, and daughter Gianna.

CHAMPIONS
adidas
NBA

Two sides of Kobe Bryant:
the furious...

...and the focused.

Excerpted from Sports Illustrated, June 7, 2010

Kobe's Final Challenge

Is he the Greatest Laker Ever? Not until he beats Boston in the Finals. Now—armed with an improved shot and fueled by a thirst for revenge—Kobe Bryant has one more chance to take down the hated Celtics

BY LEE JENKINS

The Lakers' bus left TD Garden in the middle of the night, flanked by four policemen on motorcycles, basketball's version of a funeral procession. Inside the bus it was silent, a team shell-shocked by a 39-point horse-whipping to end its season. Outside it was bedlam, a city elated by its first NBA championship in 22 years.

The Lakers were heading back to the Four Seasons at the same time revelers were pouring out of Boston bars, causing a human bottleneck in the streets. The bus was forced to stop, and as players and staff members peered out the windows, they noticed a crowd forming around them. One hand slapped the side of the bus, then another, followed by a hailstorm of hands and rocks and bottles. A security guard on the bus rushed for the door to make sure no one tried to open it. Outside, a policeman was knocked off his motorcycle. The bus was rocked back and forth until the driver finally found a clearing and the Lakers were whisked away to suffer in peace.

"It was the kind of thing," says one security official who was onboard, "that nobody forgets."

Least of all Kobe Bryant, with his elephantine memory and preternatural ability to turn failure into fuel. "It's never personal with me," Bryant says with a sarcastic grin, which of course is his way of saying that it's always personal. For a child of the 1980s who joined the Lakers before he was old enough to vote, there was perhaps nothing more personal than the loss to the Celtics in the Finals two years ago, punctuated by the 131–92 blowout in Game 6 and the bus ride in which it was rubbed in his face. "A loss like that," intones former Celtic Bill Walton, "is an indelible stain on the soul." Bryant will

Bryant dunks in Game 1 of the NBA Finals rematch against the Celtics in 2010.

not go that far, but after he beat the Celtics at TD Garden in January on a fadeaway jumper with 7.3 seconds left, he mockingly hummed the team's unofficial anthem in the shower: "I'm Shipping Up to Boston" by Dropkick Murphys. Bryant will now get a second chance to dropkick the Celtics in the Finals, with much more than revenge at stake.

It is hard to imagine that Bryant could be any more beloved in Los Angeles—when the ubiquitous Kiss Cam found actor Dustin Hoffman during the Western Conference finals, he planted a long smooch on his wife, Lisa, only to pull away and reveal a picture of Bryant wedged between their lips—but a victory over the Celtics would take him to Nicholsonian heights. Although several Lakers legends never beat the Celtics in the Finals, Bryant is surrounded by those who did: Kareem Abdul-Jabbar tutors the Los Angeles big men, Magic Johnson is a part owner, James Worthy hosts pre- and postgame TV shows, and Michael Cooper coaches the women's team down the road at USC. They are constant reminders that Bryant probably has at least one more hurdle to clear to become the Greatest Laker Ever. "It's not about beating the Celtics in the regular season," Cooper says. "You have to beat them in the playoffs. That's when you become part of the club."

Bryant has won four championships, and in all of them the Finals were an anticlimax. The more compelling matchups came in the Western Conference playoffs. That will not be the case this time, with Bryant looking for the cherry atop his legacy against the team that makes everything difficult. Boston traditionally double-covers Bryant almost every possession, and there is no reason to change, given that he is coming off the best statistical series of his career—33.7 points, 8.3 assists, and 7.2 rebounds against the Suns in the Western Conference finals. Bryant shot 52.1%, remarkable when degree of difficulty is taken into consideration, but as Lakers forward Lamar Odom puts it, "He makes the incredible normal." When Bryant iced the series in Game 6 on a double-clutch, off-balance fadeaway three near the sideline with Grant Hill tucked into his waistband, Suns coach Alvin Gentry said, "Good defense, Grant." To which Bryant replied, "Not good enough," slapping Gentry playfully on the backside.

Bryant most likely won't have many more chances at the Celtics, given their age and, to a lesser extent, his. Bryant is only 31, but NBA stars are like sports cars, in that years do not matter as much as miles. Including the playoffs, Bryant has logged 44,904 career minutes, more than Larry Bird, who played until he was 35. By the time Michael Jordan reached those minutes, he was in Washington. Bryant experienced his first real brush with basketball mortality this season, cloaked as usual in injuries to his back, knee, ankle, and hand. He sat out more games than in the previous four years combined. He acknowledged that he lost some elevation. When he scored 12 and 13 points in back-to-back first-round playoff games against the Thunder, a terrifying vision of the future flashed in front of the Lakers' eyes: Kobe Bryant, $30 million-a-year role player. "We were concerned," says Los Angeles director of athletic performance Chip Schaefer, "that he wasn't the Kobe Bryant we've all seen."

Bryant had fluid drained from his knee in the middle of the Oklahoma City series, took a few days off from practice, and then the lift in his legs returned as suddenly as it had vanished. When Bryant refers to himself as "old," stroking the nonexistent stubble on his cheeks, he is being facetious about that as well, a dig at anybody who would believe it. "The notion that I'm old and won't figure things out, that's funny to me," Bryant says. "They should know me better."

Indeed, when Father Time tried to come for him this season, he gave the old guy the middle finger.

When Chuck Person arrived in Los Angeles for training camp, he had never before said a word to Bryant. Person, a former Pacers and Kings assistant, was hired by the Lakers as a special assistant because of his close relationship with the newly acquired Ron Artest. The Lakers wanted somebody to help Artest with his transition. They did not need anybody to help Bryant with his shooting. But Person, who spent 13 years stretching NBA defenses, had studied Bryant's stroke from afar, marveling at his footwork, his vertical leap, his power of separation. "There was just one thing," Person says, "that I felt I could enhance."

A young player is taught, from the time he can lift the ball overhead, to finish the shot with his index finger pointed at the ground. "Kobe was following through with so much of the index that the ball was turning ever so slightly off that finger and he was getting a little sidespin," Person says. "When he wasn't right on, the ball would roll off the rim." Person believed he could help Bryant, but he had to be tactful about it. He could not just walk up to one of the best scorers ever and tinker with his shot. He needed an opening.

On Dec. 11 Los Angeles played the Timberwolves, and point guard Jordan Farmar made a lazy pass to Bryant at the three-point line. Timberwolves forward Corey Brewer lunged for it, deflecting the ball off Bryant's right index finger. Told he had an avulsion fracture, Bryant refused to sit out, and the next night in Utah he missed 17 of 24 shots, including eight of nine three-pointers. The time was right for Person. He approached Bryant and explained that he too had suffered an avulsion fracture in his index finger, with Indiana in 1991. He also told Bryant that the injury presented an opportunity.

"I asked him for his trust," Person says, "and I told him that we should start working together. He didn't argue with me. He bought in right away." Person wanted Bryant to put more pressure on the middle and ring fingers in his release, creating more backspin and friendlier rolls off the rim. The pad Bryant had to wear on the index finger would force him to concentrate on the other two.

The day after the Utah game, Bryant and Person convened early at the Lakers' training facility and shot for one hour before practice. The next day they did the same. Then they flew to Chicago and worked out that night at the United Center. During a break Bryant asked Person, "Did you ever score 40 points with your finger this way?" Person said he did. For Bryant it was a rare moment of self-doubt, and then it was gone. "I'm going to get 50," he said. They arrived at the United Center early the next morning for a shootaround, stayed late, and that night Bryant lit up the Bulls for 42 points on 15-of-26 shooting. A day later he scored 39 in Milwaukee, with a game-winner at the buzzer.

Penetrating Bryant's circle is not easy, but Person had a way in. As a freshman at Brantley (Ala.) High School 31 years ago, Person attended a summer basketball camp at Auburn University. The guest counselor was Jerry West, who as the Lakers executive vice president would bring Bryant from high school to Los Angeles 17 years later. "All the things I told Kobe," Person says, "are things Jerry West told me at that camp." Person persuaded Bryant to raise the ball straight into his shot instead of holding it for a moment at his hip, which has quickened his release; lift his right elbow from nose level to forehead level, which has heightened his arc; and keep that elbow pointed at the basket no matter how his body is contorted. "If you saw a tape of him shooting six months ago," Person says, "it would look completely different."

Many in the organization did not understand why Bryant insisted on playing with the broken finger. He could afford to take time off in December; they needed him healthy in

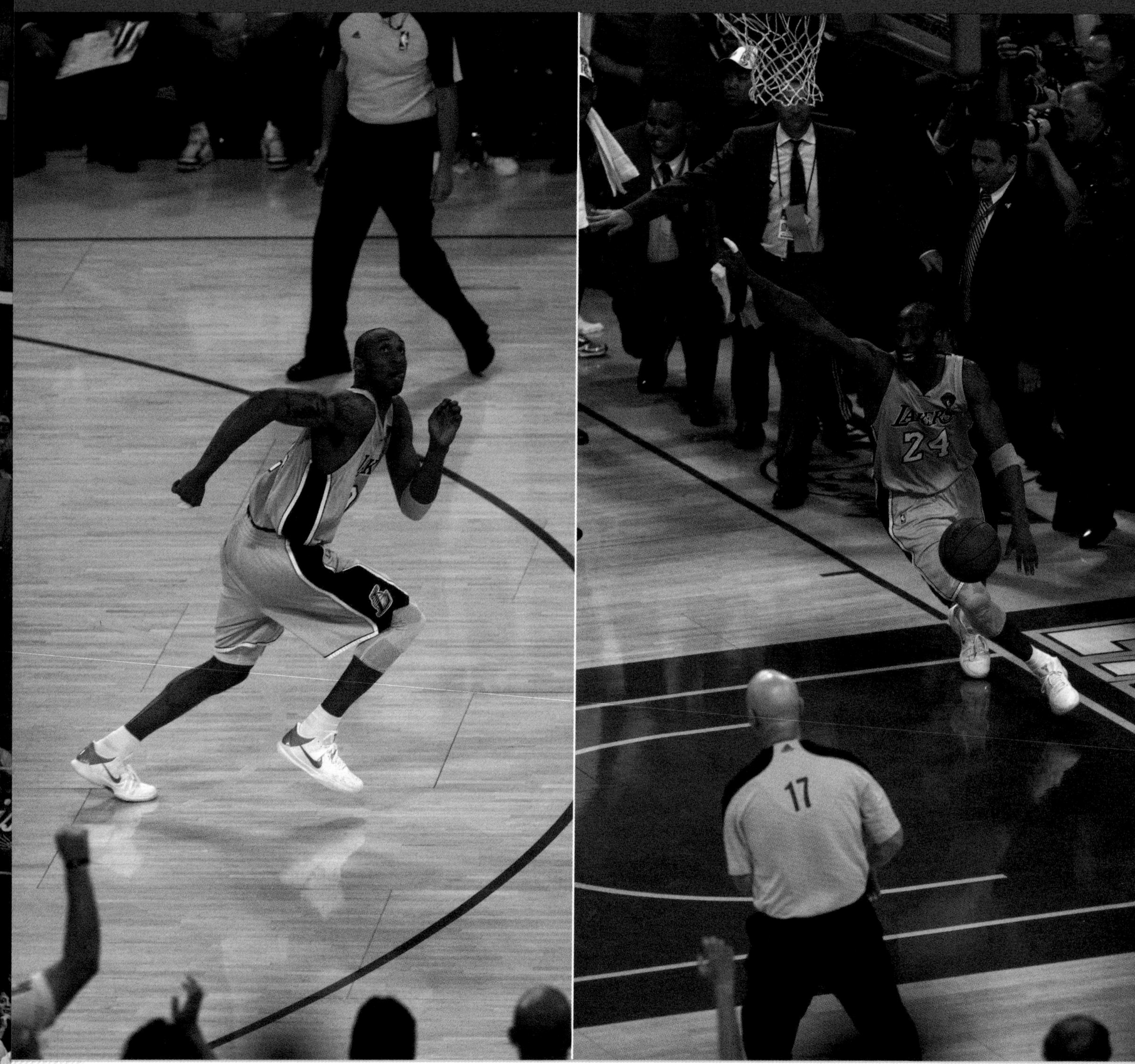

Once L.A.'s victory in Game 7 was secure, a euphoric Kobe Bryant chased down the game ball and began the celebration. Bryant scored 10 of his 23 points in the fourth quarter and grabbed several critical rebounds.

The Finals
LAKERS
24
17

2010 NBA Champions
37

Bryant and forward Ron Artest embrace after the Game 7 victory.

Bryant accepts his second straight NBA Finals MVP award.

ARTEST
LAKERS
LAKERS

2010
LAKERS

The championship celebration continued after the court was cleared, as Bryant spoke to the press alongside daughters Natalia (left) and Gianna.

Bryant looks to drive against Boston's Ray Allen in 2011. That season, Kobe was attempting to log the second three-peat of his career.

FLORIDA BLUE.COM
ampm
Too much good stuff
ampm
Too much good stuff
ampm
Too much good
105
LAKERS

Orlando Magic
1994-95
FLORIDA BLUE.COM
FLORIDA BLUE.COM
Too much good stuff
Too much good stuff
LAKERS
24
MAGIC
7
LAKERS
5
NBA WEDNESDAY
NBA SUNDAY

Excerpted from Sports Illustrated, October 21, 2013

Reflections On a Cold-Blooded Career

What does the NBA's baddest man draw upon when he's searching for the strength to get through a devastating Achilles injury? A lifetime of taking licks—beginning in a Houston dojo when he was a four-year-old—that only made him stronger

BY LEE JENKINS

Oh, no, here comes another office-park all-star with a retreating hairline and a softening middle who wants to take his pants off in front of Kobe Bryant. It is the second to last day of summer, and Bryant is sitting on a stool at the bar inside the Haute Cakes Caffe in Newport Beach, Calif., waiting for order number 18: scrambled eggs, pancakes, and a vanilla latte.

He gazes out the window into the courtyard, morning fog starting to lift on his adopted Orange County hometown, when the middle-aged man in the corner of the restaurant waves a hand. Bryant knows what the silver stranger wants to say. Part of rehab from a ruptured Achilles tendon is a hundred run-ins with Baby Boomers who underwent similar procedures after fateful pickup games and racquetball matches. They are eager to reveal the flesh evidence, regardless of what layers they must lift, unbutton, or discard. "Been 10 years," the man crows, pointing down at his own heel, "and it's never felt stronger."

Bryant does not look away, nor does he mention that he will have to cover Stephen Curry upon his return rather than Rob from marketing. He listens intently to all the tales of windsurfing expeditions and rock-climbing adventures gone awry thanks to body parts that suddenly went pop. "I love the stories," Bryant says. "It's like we're part of the same club. I call

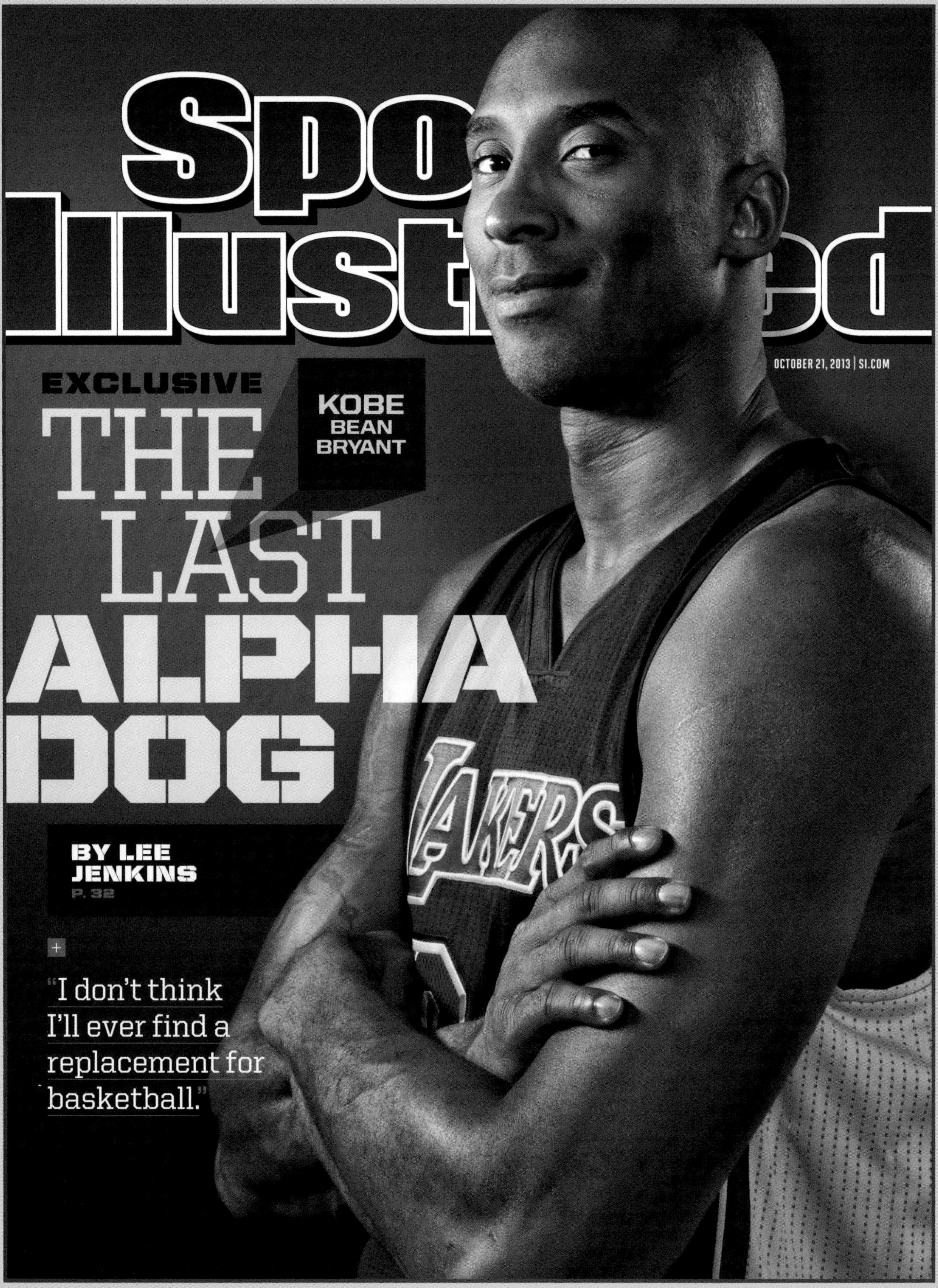

Sports Illustrated

OCTOBER 21, 2013 | SI.COM

EXCLUSIVE

KOBE BEAN BRYANT

THE LAST ALPHA DOG

BY LEE JENKINS

P. 32

+

"I don't think I'll ever find a replacement for basketball."

Bryant dunks on the Hawks at Staples Center in 2013.

these guys my scar brothers." They blush in response, turning redder than a Clippers road jersey. But Bryant doesn't sidle up to the scar brothers out of sympathy. Even the toughest s.o.b. on hardwood can use the occasional reminder that everything is going to be O.K.

More than the 31,000 points, 15 All-Star selections, and five championships, more than the silky turnaround jumpers, effortless baseline drives, and feverish scoring binges, Bryant will forever be remembered for a belief in himself that you couldn't strip with a dozen Bruce Bowens. Years ago, upon returning from the horror flick *Saw II*, Bryant described for Lakers trainer Gary Vitti a scene in which a victim awakens to find a contraption locked around his neck lined with nails pointed at his head. A videotape explains that the victim can unlock the device with a key, but it has been surgically implanted behind his right eye, and he can only extract it with a scalpel. He has a minute before it closes over his face and kills him. "I think I could get that key," Bryant said.

"I believe you," Vitti replied.

There it is, one more brushstroke applied to the intricately drawn image of Kobe Bean Bryant, so lifelike that kids ask what kind of potion he drinks on the bench, players wonder if they can bike through the desert with him in the middle of the night, and 5,000 people show up at the Nokia Theater in Los Angeles simply to watch him give Jimmy Kimmel an hourlong interview. "Everybody wants to know what's inside of him," says Lakers center Robert Sacre, who was one of the 5,000.

Coaches run Bryant as if his prime will last forever, never mind that he's 35, has cleared 54,000 minutes during the regular season and playoffs (nearly 6,000 more than Michael Jordan), and resembles a wide receiver in a league of free safeties. They say he is just different, the word observers have been using since he first fixed that fabled jaw, and therefore human limitations are easy to ignore. He doesn't flinch when an inbounds passer pretends to throw a ball at his nose. He doesn't glance down after he turns an ankle. He doesn't sleep much, content to lie with a towel over his eyes, his brain leading a fast break. When the Achilles blew, Bryant tried to manually pull the ruptured tendons down with his fingertips, so he could walk on the heel. "It's the Achilles' heel!" Vitti says. "Not even a Greek god could do that."

In an age when athletes aspire to be icons, yet share the burden of success with all their best pals, Bryant looms as perhaps the last alpha dog, half greyhound and half pit bull. No one handles him. No one censors him. He shows up alone. "What am I trying to be?" he asks. "Am I trying to be a hip, cool guy? Am I trying to be a business mogul? Am I trying to be a basketball player?" He doesn't provide an answer. He doesn't have to. It's been obvious since he was 11 years old in Italy and a club from Bologna tried to buy his rights. The gym was the place he could go at 4 a.m., "to smell the scent" and pour the fuel. Bryant wonders whether his sanctuary is finally closing, and if so, how he will cope without it. He recognizes what many around him do not: the persona, lifelike as it may be, is only partly real. Beneath it is a three-dimensional figure, with the same vulnerabilities as anybody else, plus the will to overcome them.

"I have self-doubt," Bryant says. "I have insecurity. I have fear of failure. I have nights when I show up at the arena and I'm like, 'My back hurts, my feet hurt, my knees hurt. I don't have it. I just want to chill.' We all have self-doubt. You don't deny it, but you also don't capitulate to it. You embrace it. You rise above it.... I don't know how I'm going to come back from this injury. I don't know. Maybe I'll be horses—." He pauses, as if envisioning himself as an eighth man. "Then again, maybe I won't, because no matter what, my belief is that I'm going to figure it out. Maybe not this year or even next year, but I'm going to stay with it until I figure it out."

He sips his latte. Housewives flit around the courtyard in yoga pants. A girls' basketball coach from Costa Mesa High delivers a note asking him to speak to her team, which she says needs inspiration. This must be the type of message she has in mind. Bryant slips the note into his black windbreaker.

He adopted a title for the next phase of his career, which will begin when rehab ends and he sticks that gold Lakers jersey back in his teeth, whether on opening night or Christmas Day or sometime in between. "It's The Last Chapter," Bryant says. "The book is going to close. I just haven't determined how many pages are left." He has no interest in a conversation about legacy. What excites him is evolution achieved through sports, each setback steeling a person for the next. "I'm reflective only in the sense that I learn to move forward," Bryant says. "I reflect with a purpose." Gather all his touchstones, look at them together, and they can gird the greatest player of his time for the biggest obstacle yet.

Winter of 1983 and four-year-old Kobe Bryant signs up for karate classes at a dojo in Houston. His father, Joe (Jellybean) Bryant, is playing his final NBA season, for the Rockets. Kobe is on the fast track to a yellow belt. "One day, the master of the dojo came to me and said he wanted to put me up against a brown belt," Bryant says. "I started crying. I told the master, 'That kid is so much bigger than me. He's so much better than I am.' The master said, 'You fight him!' So I stepped onto the mat, with my headgear on, my shiny red gloves. Kids were sitting all around the perimeter. I was so freaked out. I got my ass kicked, but I did get a couple of good licks in myself, and I remember sitting there at the end thinking, It wasn't as bad as I feared it would be. It wasn't as bad as I imagined. I think I realized then that your mind can wander and come up with the worst, if you let it."

Summer of 1991 and Bryant enrolls in the Sonny Hill Community Involvement League in Philadelphia. He has spent the past seven years in Italy, where Jellybean was a pro, and nobody on the club circuit overseas could stop the kid. "Then I came back here, and in that first summer I didn't score a point," Bryant says. "I'm serious. Not one point. My dad was a Philly legend. My uncle [Chubby Cox] was a Philly legend. And I'm out there with these big ol' volleyball kneepads looking like the Cable Guy. I had really bad Osgood-Schlatter disease, so even tapping my knees gave me serious pain. The league was probably 25 games, and I didn't score a basket, a free throw, nothing. At the end I sobbed my eyes out." That fall Jellybean joins a team in Mulhouse, France. The Bryant family moves into a villa with a tennis court and a basketball hoop that's 11 feet high. "Whatever, it was a hoop," Bryant says. "I played there all day long, and the only thing I thought about was, One basket, one basket, one basket. Just score one basket. When I went back to Sonny Hill the next summer, I wasn't dominating anybody, but I scored. I figured out, If you keep pushing, you'll keep getting better."

Summer of 1994 and Bryant struggles to sleep in a dorm room at Fairleigh Dickinson in Hackensack, N.J. He has earned one of the precious spots at the Adidas-sponsored ABCD camp, but he's not sure if he belongs. "I was lucky to grow up in Italy at a time when basketball in America was getting f— up with AAU shuffling players through on strength and athleticism," Bryant says. "I missed all that, and instead I was taught extreme fundamentals: footwork, footwork, footwork, how to create space, how to handle the ball, how to protect the ball, how to shoot the ball. I wasn't the strongest kid at that camp. I wasn't the fastest. I wasn't the most athletic. I was probably the most skillful, but that didn't matter. It was all about the 360 windmill dunks."

He returns to Lower Merion High in suburban Philadelphia and works out daily at 5 a.m., often alongside coach Gregg Downer, with the intention of becoming the top high school player in the U.S. "My coach used to yell,

In the later stages of his career, Bryant was forced to face numerous physical challenges, none more serious than the ruptured Achilles he suffered in 2013.

"Sometimes I shoot too much," Bryant told the team. "It's not because I don't want to pass. I don't see you at all. My mind is built on scoring. That's a weakness."

'We're steak and potatoes! We're the real thing!'" Bryant recalls. "When I went back to ABCD the next summer, I was ranked third, behind Tim Thomas and Lester Earl. I told myself, I'm not leaving this camp until I'm No. 1. I'm not leaving! Back then, if you were a highly rated player, you could stay in a nice hotel. I shacked up in the dorms. I could tell that the game meant more to me than everybody else. Other guys could leave it afterward and detach from it. I couldn't. It stuck with me. I thought about it all night.... They let players vote on who was best, and one day this kid was eating breakfast across from me. He said, 'Hey, have you seen number 143? Have you seen that kid play? He's unreal. I'm voting for him.' He didn't know it because I was so skinny, but that was me. I was 143."

Winter of 1996 and Lower Merion has a chance to win its first state championship in 53 years. Vaunted Chester High is waiting in the semifinals. "They'd already beaten us a couple of times with Kobe," Downer says. "The week of the game, our starters were competing pretty hard with the subs, and there was a collision diving for a loose ball. I look over and see Kobe lying on the floor in a pool of his own blood. All your worst fears are realized in that moment. He's got a broken nose heading into one of the most electric games in a long time. We spent a couple days frantically trying to find a mask that would fit him. The day of the game, at the Palestra, he warmed up with the mask on. But in the locker room, right before we went out on the court, he ripped it off in front of everybody. He threw it against the wall and yelled, 'I'm not wearing this thing! Let's go to war!' He scored 39 points. We won."

Three days later Lower Merion takes state.

Spring of 1997 and Bryant sits alone in the visitors' locker room at Utah's Delta Center. "Why?" he asks himself. "Why did I miss those shots? Was I nervous? No, I don't get nervous in games. I don't get afraid in games. So what happened? The shots were right on line, right on target. Why did they come up short?" He is a rookie who just unleashed three airballs down the stretch of an overtime playoff loss to the Jazz that ends the Lakers' season. He is packing for his first off-season when the answer dawns on him. "I was going from 30-something games in high school to 100-something in the NBA on an 18-year-old body," Bryant says. "I went right back to L.A. and changed my whole weight-training program. I had to start lifting during the season so what happened in Utah would never happen again." That summer

Spike Lee begins filming *He Got Game*, a movie with Denzel Washington about a basketball prodigy named Jesus Shuttlesworth. "I want you to be part of it," Lee tells Bryant. "Thank you but no thank you," Bryant says. "This summer is too big for me." Ray Allen lands the role as Shuttlesworth.

Winter of 1999 and Bryant is bracing for his third straight season coming off the bench. "I was looking at Ray Allen and Allen Iverson, guys I came into the league with, who were already starting and kicking ass," Bryant says. "I'm sitting here on the bench thinking, I'm just as good. Why aren't I playing?" Jellybean puts similar questions to Lakers general manager Mitch Kupchak, who explains the benefits of patience, but Jellybean's son is still years away from comprehending that concept. Bryant takes out his rage on the starters, punishing them in practice to prove a point. "I had to kick their ass every day," he says.

Bryant develops a penchant for dribbling through five defenders at a time, which earns him the nickname Hollywood. "That's not the name you want," cautions Lakers executive vice president Jerry West, so Bryant reduces his dribbling exhibitions and bolsters his midrange game. "On the team plane we had Shaquille O'Neal in the aisle doing the Macarena," says Del Harris, the coach of the Lakers at the time, "and Kobe watching tape of Jordan." Before the 1999 opener, small forward Rick Fox complains of sore feet because his shoe insoles don't fit properly. Bryant's days on the bench are over. No one calls him Hollywood anymore. "If I'd been allowed to start right away," he says, "who knows what would have happened to me."

Winter of 2001, Phil Jackson is the Lakers' coach, and Fox is addressing the team in a players-only meeting. "Kobe," he says, "you can do anything you want on the court, but it's like you don't need us. We want to feel like you need us." Bryant tries not to roll his eyes. You're grown-ass men, he thinks. And you're right: I don't f— need you. Then he considers the courage it took for Fox to speak up. "I had to respond," Bryant says. "I had to be as transparent with them as they were with me. I opened myself up to let them know what my insecurities are. 'Sometimes I do shoot too much. It's not because I see you open and don't want to pass. I don't see you at all. My mind is built on scoring the ball. That's a weakness. So if you're open, say something. Give me a shout....' Once your culture becomes such that your leader communicates, then everybody does the same. We still didn't hang out together off the court, but on the road we'd all go out for dinner. I learned that a lot gets accomplished over dinner and a drink."

Summer of 2004 and news breaks that O'Neal has been traded to Miami. This is great! Bryant thinks, the end of a tumultuous year in which he feuded with O'Neal, nearly signed with the Clippers, and made court appearances in Colorado for a sexual assault civil case that was later settled. "Then everything sinks in, and it's like, Oh, no, now you better win or your whole career is basically bulls—," Bryant says. "Those last three championships you won will be meaningless."

He morphs, in one off-season, from baby brother to head of household. "I was no longer a 20-year-old with 30-year-olds," Bryant says. "My teammates were suddenly my peers. I couldn't be the kid who was trying to demolish everything in his path anymore. I had to step back and realize, It's not about me, it's about you, what you're doing, goals you have, things that may be affecting you. My reputation was as this drill sergeant, and I had to make the conversion from on-court assassin to manager. But I scaled back too much. I was trying to find the balance of when to push and when to pat on the back." He calls Jordan, and they talk many times about how to impart motivation with love. "Getting other people to believe in themselves," Bryant says, "that's always been the hardest part."

Summer of 2007 and O.J. Mayo, the No. 1 high school player in the country, attends the Kobe Basketball Academy at Loyola Marymount. Mayo asks Bryant if they can work out together. "Yeah," Bryant responds, "I'll pick you up at three." The next evening Mayo sees Bryant and asks, "Where were you?" Bryant looks confused. "Three in the morning," he says. "Not three in the afternoon." Mayo slinks away. The back-patting era, however long it lasted, is over. "I can't relate to lazy people," Bryant says, speaking generally, not about Mayo. "We don't speak the same language. I don't understand you. I don't want to understand you. Go over there. If I drive somebody too hard, and he feels like he's overcommitting to the game and cracks because of it, I don't want to go to battle with him in the seventh game anyway.... Some guys don't want this. It's too much. It's too uncomfortable. If that's the case, then we can't play together. It won't work. I believe you need a confrontational crew. If I have to resort to this [shaking his head] instead of telling you that you're being lazy and f— up, then we'll never resolve anything."

Winter of 2010 and Bryant is preoccupied with the arthritic knuckle on his right index finger. He's constantly looking at it, talking about it, tweaking his shot because of it. "Why are you making such a big deal of this?" Vitti asks. Bryant silently stares him down. "Thank you," he finally says. "I needed that." He never speaks of the finger again. The Lakers win the second of their consecutive championships. Bryant, whom Vitti describes as "a McDonald's addict," celebrates by adopting a diet in which he eliminates junk food.

Spring of 2013 and Bryant lies on a table in the training room at Staples Center, his wife's lipstick on his cheek and tears in his eyes. "He was having that moment of doubt," Vitti says. "You could see it. It was all going through his head: I'm going to be 35, 17 years in the league, and this isn't a sprained ankle. I've ruptured the Achilles. Normally, that's when guys start getting different opinions and going through a decision-making process and wondering if they will ever come back." Patrick Soon-Shiong, a surgeon and one of the team's minority owners, walks in and says, "You should have surgery tomorrow." Bryant is still wearing his uniform. "Yeah," he agrees. "Let's do it tomorrow."

Two weeks and two days later, the Lakers host the Spurs in Game 4 of the first round of the playoffs, and Bryant changes outfits in the locker room. He needs five minutes to pull his pant leg over the cumbersome boot on his left foot. As he limps out, center Dwight Howard cruises in. "What the f— is going on?" Bryant asks a trainer. "Dwight got ejected," he is informed. In the retelling, Bryant waits eight seconds to utter another word, looking as if he might literally bite his tongue. "Sports have a funny way of doing s— like that," he says.

L.A. is about to be swept and Howard is about to leave for Houston, where he will forfeit $30 million and avoid discomfort. But Bryant is the rare modern athlete whose presence can transcend playoff results and free-agent decisions. Sometimes, just seeing him is enough. "The long year, the injuries, the Shaq stuff, the Phil stuff, it all came to a head when I walked out to the bench," says Bryant, who was serenaded with a standing ovation and MVP chants. "It was the first time I ever felt that kind of love from a crowd. Oh, my God, I was fighting back the tears."

Summer of 2013 and he is gripping a towel with the toes of his left foot. The Lakers' weight room is empty except for Bryant, shirtless in camouflage shorts, and Judy Seto, the physical therapist who has been kneading his muscles for the past 15 years. On the end of the towel is a circular 2½-pound silver weight. Bryant clenches the foot to inch the weight toward him. Then he does it again. Soon, he will graduate to picking up marbles with his toes and placing them in a jar. Shortly after surgery Bryant called

> **"I don't know how I'm going to come back. Maybe I'll be horses—. Then again, I'm going to stay with it until I figure it out."**

several players whose careers were threatened or cut short by ruptured Achilles tendons. Pistons guard Chauncey Billups advised Bryant to be meticulous with the rehab, the reps, but at some point his voice trailed off. Telling Kobe to be meticulous is like telling Will Ferrell to be funny. "Some people would get bored by this," Bryant says. "I don't get bored."

The weight-room television plays a highlight of Mariano Rivera, in his last season with the Yankees, striking out a Met. Years ago Jerry West told Bryant, "Don't play beyond your time," but now Bryant is asking the inevitable follow-up: "How do you know when it's your time? How do you know?" He put that question to the recently retired David Beckham. "You just know," Beckham replied.

Bryant has started the search for another place to pour the fuel. When he hears about a project or company that intrigues him, he calls the president and asks to meet. "I'm learning," he says. "That's where I am. I don't think I'll ever find a replacement for basketball. But you have to find something else you're passionate about." It's hard to conceive of a sports world where Kobe Bryant doesn't drive the daily conversation, with a sound bite, a sideways glance, or a flight to Germany, where he jetted early this month for another round of platelet-rich plasma therapy on his troublesome right knee. He scans his elephantine memory for another NBA immortal who left at the right moment. He is quiet for a while. "Bill Russell," he says. Bill Russell had 11 championships.

Bryant will play again, and play well, because he has unknowingly spent three decades preparing for the final stage of his basketball life. On road trips to Philadelphia he often shows up before dawn at the Lower Merion gym, and Downer once found him launching nothing but floaters. "Dikembe Mutombo blocked my shot," Bryant explained. "That will never happen again." He let another teardrop lick the sky. He has been expanding a repertoire he can channel when the reverse layups are gone.

"Maybe I won't have as much explosion," Bryant says. "Maybe I'll be slower. Maybe I'll lose quickness. But I have other options. It's like Floyd Mayweather in the ring. There's a reason he's still at the top after all these years. He's the most fundamentally sound boxer of all time. He can fight myriad styles at myriad tempos. He can throw fast punches or off-speed punches, and he can throw them from odd angles."

Those close to Bryant worry less about his return than the issues that could arise afterward.

Last season the Lakers failed to win a playoff game despite a ballyhooed starting lineup with four potential Hall of Famers. The remaining three are now well into their 30s—Bryant, point guard Steve Nash (39), and center Pau Gasol (33)—and coming off injuries. Nash is suffering from a sore left ankle; Gasol is recovering from tendinitis in both knees; Bryant is not in basketball shape and has yet to practice. The Lakers can't tank, not with Bryant on the roster, but they aren't exactly scaring the Spurs with the sale-rack additions of Nick Young, Wesley Johnson, and Chris Kaman. Though coach Mike D'Antoni will unearth ways to score, it's hard to imagine how the Lakers stop anybody.

"It can't be tougher than last season," Bryant says of a year in which he averaged 27.3 points, matched a career high with 6.0 assists, and shot the best effective field-goal percentage of his career, single-handedly ensuring that L.A. at least avoided the ignominy of missing the playoffs. But the team is essentially biding time until July, when Bryant's maximum contract comes off the books, along with Gasol's. Bryant is fiercely loyal to the Lakers, and they to him, but neither knows what to expect from the other. "We're going to have to wait and see," says GM Kupchak. "It's a blank slate." Maybe Bryant re-signs for a discount price and recruits two bedrock free agents next summer, when LeBron James, Carmelo Anthony, and others can opt out of existing deals. But it's more likely that James and Anthony stay put or go elsewhere, in which case the Lakers' future becomes hazy, and Bryant's as well. Is he really picking up marbles with his toes so he can spearhead a rebuilding project?

Bryant did not shoot a basketball from April to September, the longest break he can remember, and he was surprisingly content. He watched a lot of *Modern Family* ("I'm Phil," he says) with his wife and two daughters. He took up scuba diving. He drove the girls to club soccer games. Natalia, 10, smiles on the field like Magic Johnson. Gianna, 7, acts more like her father. "She doesn't look at you," Bryant says. "She's there to kick your butt."

Gianna's team lost a game recently, and she cried afterward. Standing on the sideline Bryant studied her, pained but proud. "Sports are such a great teacher," he says. "I think of everything they've taught me: camaraderie, humility, how to resolve differences. Playing with Shaq made me understand that you're never going to change a person. You have to work with his position." He would be a hell of a coach if he could find more players who suited him, more Giannas.

"Hey," he told her, after the tears dried. "You want to see Daddy cry?" He took her home and fished out the DVD from Game 6 of the 2008 Finals. They sat together and watched the Lakers get mortified in Boston. Then he popped in Game 7 of the 2010 Finals, and they marinated in the vindication. There, in one unforgettable double feature, was the evolution, the making of a man, the healing of a scar.

A jubilant Bryant celebrates his fifth and final championship, in 2010.

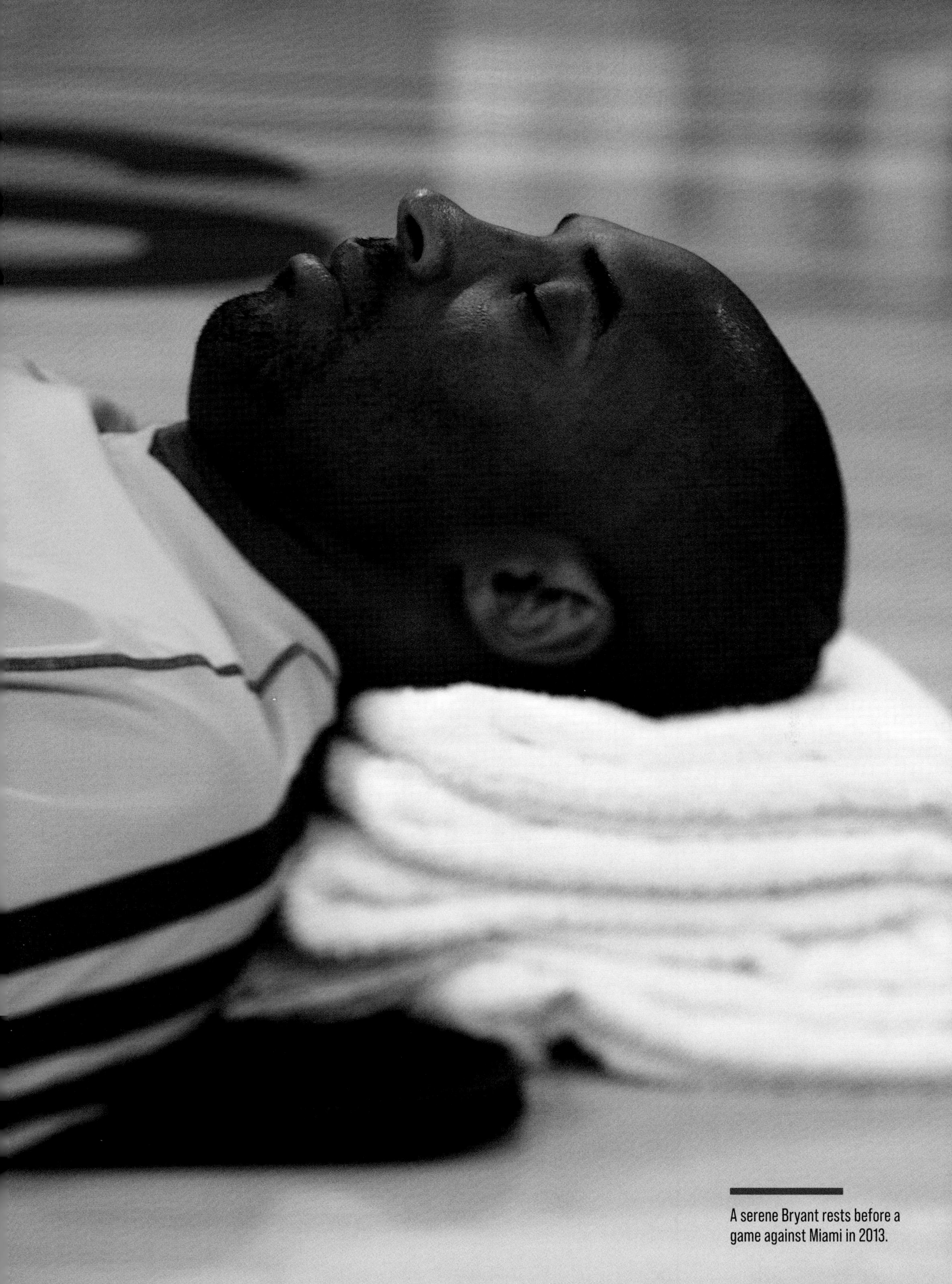

A serene Bryant rests before a game against Miami in 2013.

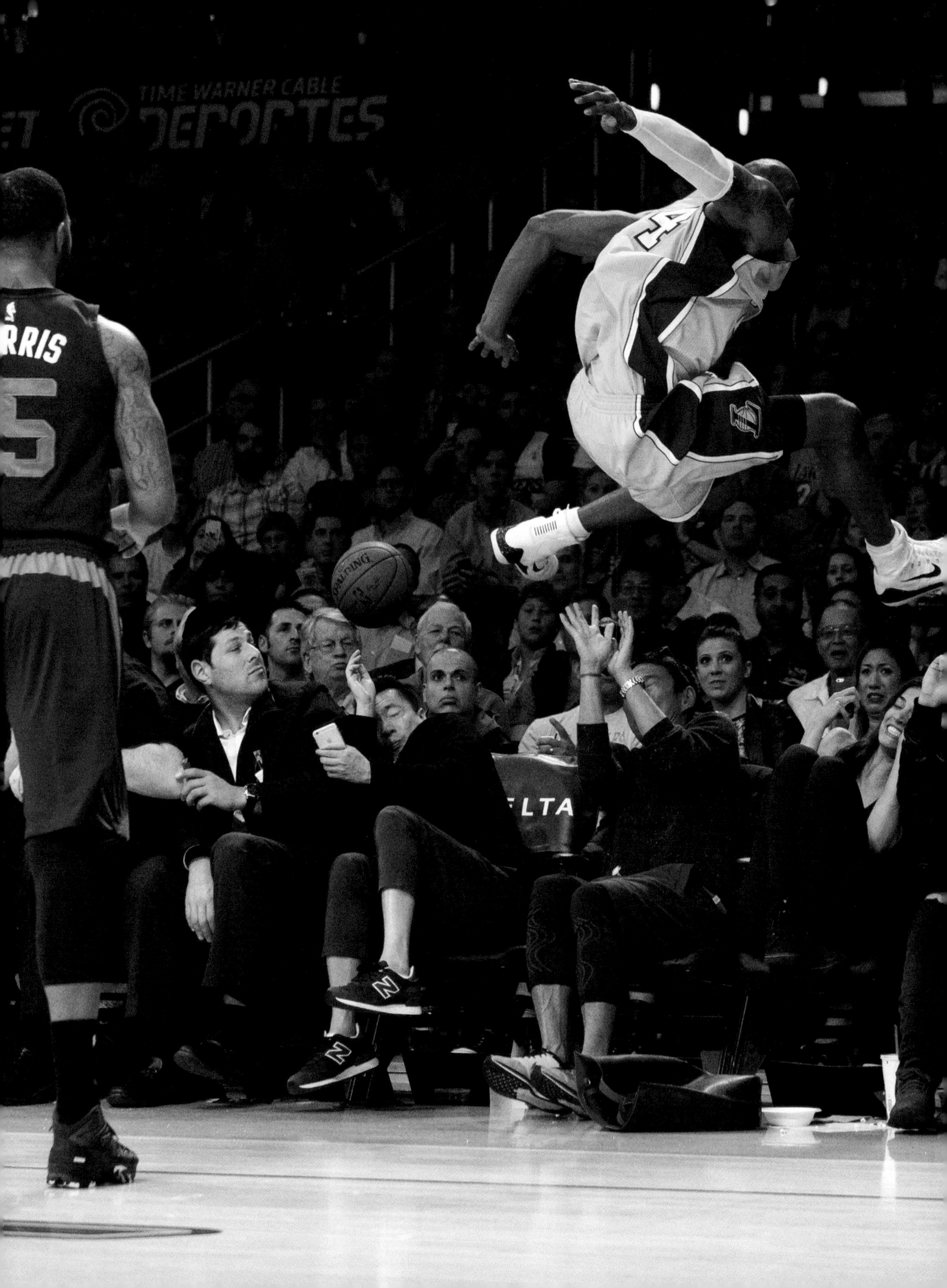
TIME WARNER CABLE
DEPORTES
RRIS
ELTA

A repaired Achilles would not stop Bryant from going all out to chase a loose ball.

Excerpted from Sports Illustrated, August 25, 2014

Twilight the Saga

The final, fascinating days of a legend (and a stray journeyman)

BY CHRIS BALLARD

You might pity the many NFL veterans listed as "unsigned free agents," or empathize with Giants running back David Wilson, who recently announced through tears that a neck injury was ending his career. But such hard cases come with a slim silver lining. At least the decision is made for those players, and they won't have to confront this central dilemma: When do I retire?

There's no right time for the deeply personal decision of when to power down a career. Some athletes lick the bottom of the bowl, savoring every last drop of the experience. Others have a lower threshold for decline. And then there are the legions—Michael Jordan, Brett Favre, most boxers worth their mouthpieces—who find that retirement isn't working, as it were, and rejoin the fray.

But even the most competitive athlete (that's you, Kobe Bryant) must confront The End, and its attendant changes in earning power, lifestyle, physique, and purpose. SI visited with Bryant and four other athletes in their autumn years as they ponder when to say when.

The thick-armed man moves quickly, establishing a perimeter and securing the entryway. This is his seventh year on Kobe Bryant's overseas security team, and he knows how quickly things can go sideways, especially in China. Once, four years ago in Shandong Province, a guy slept overnight on the roof of a gym, curled in the darkness, and then, when Kobe approached, leaped from a low overhang, yelling, "Kohhhh-beeee!" In one fluid motion Attila Portik—for that is the muscle-bound man's name, of Hungarian origin—intercepted the crazed fan and hurled him aside, as if bailing out a boat. Another time the mob breached the perimeter and swarmed in, so close someone ripped out Bryant's earring. Just a year ago teenagers in Shanghai scaled police cars to get a view. The cops didn't stop them; they too were trying to see. Now Attila and his counterpart, a buzz-cut L.A. police officer named Robert Lara, insist on metal

Kobe Bryant | Roger Federer | Michael Phelps | Becky Hammon | Nick Punto

Twilight *the* Saga

+ THE FINAL, FASCINATING DAYS OF A LEGEND

Sports Illustrated

(And a Stray Journeyman)
By
CHRIS BALLARD
P. 48

PLUS

The Mo'ne Masterpiece
BY
ALBERT CHEN
P. 4

"I'm 70 In Basketball Years."

KOBE BRYANT

barricades and use decoy cars. You have not seen hysteria, Attila explains, until you've seen Kobe in China.

On this late-July afternoon, fans have been massing for hours in the humid air outside Jiangwan Stadium, here in the northeast part of Shanghai, amid the high-rises and the smog and the clamor. They arrive wearing Kobe jerseys and shirts that read RING COLLECTOR and 24 ON THE FLOOR. They carry poster boards and giant banners. One reads PRAY FOR KOBE, above a photo of Bryant holding his cracked kneecap. Another reads FOREVER YOUNG, with the tagline TO THE GREAT FATHER, EXCELLENT PLAYER. Two nearby outdoor basketball courts are polka-dotted with yellow-and-purple number 24 jerseys—short, skinny Kobes driving on chubby Kobes before passing to wiry, bespectacled Kobes. Nearby, vendors hawk homemade KOBE hats and BLACK MAMBA temporary tattoos. Conspicuously, no one wears generic Lakers gear. They do not care about the team, only Kobe. He is like a cross between Justin Bieber and Neo from *The Matrix*.

At 5:45 p.m. the riot cops arrive, wearing helmets and toting shields and long metal poles that end in U-shaped curves wide enough to corral a man's neck. By 6:30 the street is clogged with gold jerseys. Fans climb lampposts and scramble up trees. Some have tickets for tonight's event; others will wait more than five hours just to see Kobe walk into a building.

Just after sundown it happens. A black van with tinted windows pulls through the iron gates. The mob, thousands strong, begins pogoing up and down, emitting a guttural noise. Koohhhh-beeee! Kooohhh-bee! The riot cops tense, ready to hold the line. And now Bryant emerges, wearing a white T-shirt and shorts. This is his ninth visit to China in the last 15 years, but he is still surprised every time he sees the fervor anew. So Bryant waves and moves quickly, striding up the stairs and into the gym, past a row of purple spotlights and two life-sized statues of himself in mid-dunk and into what was once a gymnasium but for the week has been remade by Nike into something that can only be described as a temple, unironically dubbed the House of Mamba. Striding past the wall-sized rack of purple basketballs, down a hall lined with giant inspirational Kobe quotes and trailed by a team of nearly a dozen handlers, Bryant is directed to a room marked VVIP. There he is outfitted with a microphone headset and transponders on each triceps. In the next three hours he will preside over a bizarre basketball TV show, part *American Idol*, part *The Hunger Games*, part Terry Gilliam fever dream, that is held on an LED-lit court while Chinese emcees scream in Mandarin and young women weep. And then, at night's end, Bryant will, to the shock and dismay of his handlers, go off-script and challenge a Chinese teenager to a full-court game of one-on-one on his rebuilt knee and Achilles, footage of which will later leak onto the Web. Afterward, a young man in a 24 jersey will leap from the stands and literally prostrate himself in front of Bryant, hands clasped together in prayer to a roundball deity.

And this is only Kobe's first day in China.

Back in the States, if all goes as planned, Bryant will, a little more than two months from now, jog down a tunnel in Staples Center, acknowledge a cheering crowd, and play in his first NBA game since fracturing his left knee last December. It will mark his 19th season in the league, a career during which time he has won five titles and one MVP award, and logged more minutes than all but 12 men in NBA history. Barring any transactional miracles, his most-talented teammates this season will be Carlos Boozer, Jeremy Lin, and Julius Randle. Naturally, Bryant is certain that this makeshift crew is capable of greatness. "I hear people say, 'They don't have a championship team,'" Bryant said a week earlier, while peering out an eighth-floor window at the Beverly Hills Hilton. "Yeah, maybe from your perspective"—and here Bryant pauses, narrows his eyes—"but Boozer does this, Jordan Hill does that, Lin adds that. What's the best way to put all these pieces together and use them to win? That's the puzzle to figure out, and if we can figure out that puzzle, we'll shock a lot of people." Bryant was at the Hilton on this afternoon to promote an upcoming Showtime documentary called *Kobe Bryant's Muse*, for which he is an executive producer. He'd just finished sitting on a media panel alongside a Showtime exec and the film's director, Gotham Chopra. Almost immediately a reporter veered off topic and asked about the Lakers' future. And then about LeBron. The Showtime guy cut off the question, snapping, "You're not wasting [any more of] our time." But Bryant waved him off. He understands that people only care about the movie because they care about his career. As he put it, "That's part of the entire damn story."

Now, up in a sprawling eighth-floor banquet room with views of the Hollywood hills, Bryant continues to talk optimistically about what's to come. His confidence is as admirable as it is predictable. And yet on paper the Lakers look an awful lot like a lottery team that is overly reliant on one aging star. There is not much hope on the horizon, either. Seven months after he ruptured his left Achilles tendon—and three weeks before he fractured the left knee—Bryant signed a $48.5 million, two-year deal. The contract, widely derided as the worst in the game, makes Bryant nearly impossible to move, even were the Lakers to try. Asked about Kobe's value on the market, one GM answers definitively: "Zero. Look at that number. Who takes him?"

This is by design, of course. It ensures that Bryant accomplishes something very few modern athletes have: playing an entire career with one team. Bryant's plan is to retire in two years, though he says he reserves the right to change his mind. Thus one of the game's greatest players and one of its two fiercest competitors—Michael Jordan being the other—will likely exit the league laboring for an undermanned squad in a stacked conference. It seems wrong. Never the type for farewell tours, Bryant bristles at the idea of parading from arena to arena, receiving parting gifts and teary-eyed salutes. "No, no, no, no, I'm good," he says, waving his hands. "If you booed me for 18, 19 years, boo me for the 20th. That's the game, man."

But most of them won't boo. Much as happens with other sports villains in their later years, fans have warmed to Bryant. It helps that in his latest iteration he has become the truthsayer of the NBA, the closest there is to Charles Barkley among the playing ranks, ready to tell it like it is. Most people hit the f-it stage of life at age 70 or 75. Bryant, who will turn 36 shortly after returning to the States, appears to have arrived there already. ("It's because I'm 70 in basketball years," he jokes.)

Eighteen months is a long time, though. Before his Achilles injury, he was an MVP candidate and the Lakers had Dwight Howard and Pau Gasol. Now? Now he's teamed with Nick Young and Wesley Johnson while the national conversation centers around KD and LeBron and Kevin Love.

Bryant understands this, even if he won't abide it. This may be "the finale of my career," as he calls it, but he intends to go out as he came in, guns firing. Still, as he prepares for the comeback from his comeback, Bryant has become more introspective. He is interested in his place in the game, in documenting his life. He wants to disseminate what he's learned. To spread the gospel of Kobe. Which helps explain why he has come to China.

At 8:25 a.m. on Bryant's second day in Shanghai, he walks into the near-empty gym on the fourth floor of the towering Shangri-La hotel in west Shanghai. Seeing a reporter, he smiles, saying, "So you made it out after all." And with that, Bryant begins one of his legendary workouts.

He starts on the stationary bike, which he rides leisurely for 15 minutes, staring out the window through a light drizzle at the morning traffic on the Yan'an Elevated Road. Then it's on to some leg extensions, followed by bodyweight exercises. Throughout, Bryant keeps up a running conversation with his good friend and Nike account manager, Nico Harrison, an easygoing former Montana State forward. Some of Kobe's favorite topics of conversation include: what Bryant read on Techcrunch the night before, the latest news on Buzzfeed, and whether Katy Perry is a genius businesswoman or just a plain genius. (Bryant has been a longtime admirer of Perry's and was nervous when he met her for the first time recently, when both happened to be dining at Chateau Marmont in Los Angeles.) At one point Bryant even appears to break a sweat.

This is the dirty little secret that becomes apparent while spending a week around Bryant in Shanghai: he is human. He does not wake at 2 a.m. to run wind sprints through the streets of the city. He does not spend three hours a day doing visualization exercises while chanting samurai mantras. And sometimes his workout in a hotel gym is pretty much the same as the workout you or I would do in a hotel gym. This is the reality of being 35 years old, with the legs of a 45-year-old.

While he retains his superhuman tolerance—"He has the highest pain threshold I've ever seen," says his longtime physical therapist, Judy Seto—even Bryant knows that he can only push so far. He is coming off two significant injuries. His body needs to rest. Recently he saw a top nutritionist, hoping to find some magic diet that would restore his energy to its earlier levels, as if aging is but a matter of changing your carbs-to-protein ratio. "There are certain things that my body can't do that I used to be able to do," Bryant admits. "And you have to be able to deal with those. First you have to be able to figure out what those are. Last year when I came back, I was trying to figure out what changed. And that's a very hard conversation to have." Bryant pauses. "So when I hear the pundits and people talk, saying, 'Well, he won't be what he was.' Know what? You're right! I won't be. But just because something evolves, it doesn't make it any less better than it was before."

Kobe's focus these days is on efficiency. Over the summer he's trained nearly every day, either at the Lakers' facility or at a gym near his house in Orange County. Sometimes he'll have a partner join him for drills—often Johnson, the 27-year-old Lakers small forward. In these instances Bryant takes on a mentoring role, pointing out Johnson's wasted steps and where he can be more effective. Other times Bryant works out by himself, except for two ball boys, shooting and sweating for up to two hours, never talking. His goal is to regain his conditioning—after adding some body fat earlier in the year, he now looks almost frail with his shirt off. The end goal, of course, is to evolve. "I'll be sharper," he says. "Much sharper. Much more efficient in areas. I'll be limited in terms of what you see me do, versus a couple years ago. But very, very methodical, very, very purposeful."

On this morning in Shanghai, his hotel workout is certainly purposeful. He is done within an hour. Bryant heads to his room to get ready. Today is Design Day. Kobe has been to China so many times now that he has done all the tourist stuff. So a young Nike rep was tasked with putting together an itinerary of unusual experiences, broken down by theme. Yesterday was Greatness Day, followed by Design Day, and tomorrow, when Nike has arranged to close down a local museum, is Art Day.

Bryant's black luxury van arrives in the early afternoon in the trendy M50 neighborhood, where he meets an artist-designer named Zhang Zhoujie, who has been given Nikes to wear for the occasion. Zhang, a thin, nervous man in white jeans and wide-frame glasses, uses a computer to individually map each chair he

"You know how it's been hard for Jordan in retirement?" says one GM. "It's going to be way worse to be Kobe. At least MJ likes to golf and play cards."

designs so no two are alike. His personal narrative appeals to Bryant: Turned down by studios, Zhang spent four years teaching himself how to produce the chairs. Now he sells them for 10 grand apiece and recently held a show in L.A., from which he returned with bags of official Kobe gear for his friends. Now he is meeting the actual man in the flesh, and he is having a hard time keeping it together. Tentatively, he presents a slide show to Bryant, who appears genuinely curious, putting his finger on his chin and nodding seriously, asking questions throughout. Bryant asks about process, about production scale. Asked to sit on the $10,000 chair, Bryant lowers himself slowly, then says, "This might be the most comfortable chair I've ever sat in. Seriously"—and here he motions at Nico—"you gotta try this."

This side of Kobe, the inquisitive entrepreneur, is a relatively new development. Early in his rehab from the knee injury, he was limited to 45 minutes a day on the exercise bike, which left him 23 hours and 15 minutes to focus on something other than basketball. It was hell. "You get this feeling that you're living without a purpose," says Bryant. "And that's not O.K." So Bryant watched *Modern Family* with his kids and read business tomes and spent long hours talking with people he admires and filling a series of notebooks. He's on his fourth now. "Just nothing but sketches and drawing and org charts and direction and all this s—. Conversations I've had with muses, how they built their company, notes and all kinds of s—." (One of Bryant's conversational fallbacks is swearing in situations where swearing doesn't necessarily seem warranted. It is a way to soften himself, an attempt to bridge the gap he assumes exists when talking to people unlike himself.)

Of late, Bryant has become obsessed with obsessives, and he devours biographies of iconoclasts. Often he'll divulge some factoid like, "Did you know that Leonardo da Vinci didn't break onto the art scene until he was 46 years old? Forty-six?!?" Bryant recently cold-called Apple exec Jonathan Ive and Oprah Winfrey, among others, asking for business advice. He is curious in a manner most athletes aren't. He wants to know how and why things work. Last year he formed Kobe Inc., hiring away creative talents he admired from companies he'd worked with. (Bryant, who got this killer instinct from his strong-willed mother, hired Andrea Fairchild, formerly of Gatorade, as his CEO.) Among those Bryant idolizes—Steve Jobs and Bruce Lee, for instance—there is often a common theme. They are outsiders. They buck the system. Succeed against the odds. In their lives Bryant sees not just road maps but validation.

Earlier this year Bryant heard a story about Michael Jackson, another of his idols. It was about how, before *Thriller* came out, Jackson was obsessed with the Bee Gees, and in particular their *Saturday Night Fever* soundtrack, which was then the best-selling album of all time. Determined to eclipse the Bee Gees, Jackson began listening to *Saturday Night Fever* over and over. Such was his obsession that for two years straight, Jackson told friends, he listened to the album 10 times a day, until he knew every note, every beat. Until he'd internalized it, deciphered its magic, and taken it for his own. A year later *Thriller* came out. It sold more than 60 million copies and became the best-selling album of all time.

When Bryant first heard this anecdote, he was ecstatic. "I f— love that story," Bryant said. Here, crystallized, was everything Bryant held dear: the value of work ethic and passion and obsessive quests, all doused in mythology. Did Jackson actually listen to *Saturday Night Fever* 10 times a day, or was it more like five? Did he do it for two years, or two months? These were not questions Bryant asked. Better to build up a myth than tear it down.

The man who told Bryant that story about Michael Jackson was 39-year-old director Gotham Chopra. The son of New Age guru Deepak Chopra, Gotham grew up amid his own surreal media bubble: on TV as a boy, shot by paparazzi as a teen, published author while still in college. His childhood was as surreal as Bryant's, if in a different way. (He met Jackson through his father and became good friends with him as a teen.)

Kobe and Gotham met two years ago, through a mutual friend, and first bonded over comic books. Bryant was interested in documenting his comeback from an Achilles injury. Gotham, a personable man with big brown eyes—and a die-hard Celtics fan, something which Kobe loves to needle him about—signed on, even though the project was nebulous. "Hey, if Kobe wants you to film, you film," he says.

Then Kobe's knee buckled, and the movie had to become about something else. So it became about Kobe's inspiration—his "muses" as Bryant calls them. Gotham has now spent roughly 60 days with Bryant over the course of more than a year. He has reams and reams of footage. The movie is slated to premiere on Nov. 7, soon after Kobe's return.

Like any auteur, Chopra wants to make a revealing film. Which means he is in a difficult position. A lifetime spent in front of cameras—a lifetime of creating personas and reinforcing them, of burnishing his own mythology, just as Michael Jackson once did—makes it hard for Kobe to let down his guard, even when he tries. At one point I ask Bryant why he has yet to sign on for a ghost-written autobiography. He says he's thought about it. That he's read Andre Agassi's book and admires it. But if he did it, Bryant says, he'd want to actually write the book himself. Even so, he says, "I'm not ready yet. Writing carries such a level of transparency. I think if you're going to write a book, you have to be ready to be completely transparent about everything that's taken place. And I'm not at that place yet."

For now Bryant often speaks in parables, all of which have roughly the same moral: never give up, and if you work hard, you will succeed. In interviews and at basketball camps and in speeches, again and again, he tells the same stories: about that summer in Philly where, as a wiry kid, he failed to score during the entirety of the Sonny Hill summer league. ("Zero points!") And the one about how at four years old he was forced to fight an older, better kid at karate and got his ass kicked only to realize he'd survived and was now stronger for it. Such are his charisma and social skills—dramatizing big moments, enunciating key words—that he makes each story feel new and insightful, the way a skilled politician can. "Somebody told me, When you go to China, you'll see people really respond to his teachings," Chopra says with a laugh. "Kobe has teachings?"

The Kobe Way can be applied to any endeavor. When he spoke recently with one of his various Kobe Inc. partners, a moment caught by Gotham on film, Bryant groused about "this thing where we seem to be O.K. for kids to receive medals for fourth place.... It's bull—." Instead Kobe wants to use his company to foster, as he calls it, "the spirit of competition." At home, Bryant drills his eight-year-old daughter on winning, only he calls it "competing." The lesson remains the same: sometimes you lose, but when you do, it just reminds you of how much you like to win. Says Chopra, "Sometimes I tell Kobe, You've obviously been successful. Whatever you've done seems to have worked. But this losing/winning mentality you have, where everything is a competition? In basketball, yes. Maybe even in business, yes. But parenting, not so much. Relationships? There's compromise. At least that's my experience. But, you know, he kind of hasn't had to till now." (At one point Gotham introduced his seven-year-old son to Kobe. Afterward, Bryant turned to Gotham and said, "I'm thinking of creating one of those," as if a son were a product.)

At this point, Bryant has institutionalized his mentality. Again and again over the week, he repeats his mantras, telling the Chinese kids to "be strong" and "learn from failure" and "never stop working to get better." Here is the thing: Bryant encourages these kids to grow from weakness, but he never shows any himself. You know how Kobe deals with a torn Achilles? He tries to pull the damn thing up, then stays in the game to take, and make, two free throws. Aging? Kobe has publicly scoffed at the notion that Father Time is undefeated. Armed with a roster of Lins and Boozers, Kobe says he's thinking championship. And he really does buy into this stuff. "First of all, I'm sure he believes they can make the playoffs," says one GM. "And second of all, I'm sure he believes it will be on his shoulders. That's what makes him Kobe. That unnatural confidence."

Now it's Day 3 of Bryant's visit, and he's back at the House of Mamba, filming. The online reality show is the brainchild of Nike, though it is full of Kobe's input, of course. Everything you see involving Kobe includes his input; hence his line of shoes named after people he admires, including the Bruce Lee, the Beethoven, and the Thriller.

The TV show is essentially one long, overt Nike advertisement, part of a concentrated effort by both athletic companies and the NBA to make China the next frontier for basketball. (The league is developing a 130,000-square-foot structure in Beijing, and commissioner Adam Silver recently said he sees the country as a key to the NBA's continued growth.) In Nike's case the company solicited 30-second video clips from teenagers across China, then chose the most interesting. During Week 1, LeBron James came through and narrowed the field down to 30. Now Kobe will narrow that field to 10. Despite the star power and relevancy of James, Attila says there is no comparison when it comes to popularity. He has spent nearly a decade on Asian security detail for NBA stars and watched over LeBron just the week before. "You can tell one is trying to get where the other is," Attila says. Asked if he means there are more fans for Kobe, he nods. "Lots more."

On this afternoon Kobe tutors the players on specific skills. He is exacting but patient, showing a chubby, big-eared kid how to shoot a fadeaway from the right post, a shot that this kid should probably not even consider taking until he's mastered more rudimentary moves. Still, Kobe sticks with him as he flubs shot after shot. "Fake left, shoot it over your right shoulder," Bryant says. "Don't use the dribble." The kid tries again and makes the shot. Kobe is happy. He is clearly a good teacher. Though he says he has no interest in coaching, he would be a good one. If he had the patience for it.

The Chinese teenagers, chosen by Nike as much for their backstories as their skill, need plenty of help. A handful might qualify as D-III players in the U.S. Many wouldn't make a high school JV squad. There are no Yao Ming–esque giants. Most hew closer to the Jeremy Lin model: quick on the dribble, attack the basket, suspect jumper, pass-second.

This last element becomes magnified when Kobe is watching. Over the course of the week, the contestants rotate through half-court five-on-five games. When Bryant is near, whichever kid has the ball invariably backs up and waves away his teammates, then goes one-on-five and attempts a crazy finish. Doing his best to be diplomatic, Bryant offers encouragement. "That's some good D!" he says.

Ostensibly, the hysterical fans who arrive during the week are there to cheer on the reality show, but they couldn't care less about these teenagers. Rather, they wait for Bryant to turn in their direction, at which point they raise their banners and their light-up MVP signs and scream their throats out. Every minute or so they break into spontaneous KOH-BEE! chants. For two hours. It looks exhausting.

In the U.S., or many other places, there would be an acknowledgement of the show's naked marketing, an eye-rolling, snark-soliciting acquiescence by those on hand. Not here. Here they eat it up. Jake Bloch, Gotham's 25-year-old producer, who happens to be half Chinese, refers to it as China's "preironic" mind-set. When Kobe signs basketballs at the end of one taping and throws them to the crowd, scrums break out as dozens of teens grapple and fall and tear at the leather. It is disturbing. Like *Lord of the Flies*. At one point during the taping of the show, a girl plays the trumpet for Kobe, one-handed, while dribbling a basketball, and the song is Celine Dion's "My Heart Will Go On," the romantic ballad from *Titanic*.

Amid everything else, it seems totally normal.

Why does China love Kobe? Why does Kobe love China?

The answer on both fronts might be that it's uncomplicated. In an autocratic country, the very idea of Bryant may be liberating. He represents the best of the West, Easternized: the validation of work ethic as the path to success. If he so chose, after his retirement from the NBA, Bryant could easily spend his golden years holding clinics in China. Like David Hasselhoff in Germany, only taller and less cheesy.

As for Kobe, here in China he really is, as the sign reads, FOREVER YOUNG. Here the local media dotes. The fans not only adore him but arrive with no expectations beyond glimpsing the icon. Hang around a Lakers' road hotel in the U.S., and you'll see groupies and autograph hounds awaiting the bus, and if the players don't acknowledge them, angry 40-year-old men will

> **Bryant bristles at the idea of parting gifts and teary-eyed salutes: "If you booed me for 18, 19 years, boo me for the 20th. That's the game, man."**

berate them. In Shanghai, I saw one group of nearly a dozen teenagers outside the Shangri-La hotel at 10 in the morning one day; at 11:30 p.m. they were still there, waiting, hopeful, asking any Westerner who entered if they knew when Kobe might return. They carried a succession of handwritten placards, in English, one holding each, that read KOBE CAN WE TAKE PHOTO WITH U? [heart].

This kind of unconditional love is rare. Growing up, Kobe received it, like most kids, from his parents. Now he gets it from Chinese 17-year-olds.

Kobe's relationship with his father is complicated. Joe Bryant was a good NBA player and an exceptional international one, a power forward who played with panache. But Kobe sees little of his father in himself. "We couldn't be more opposite, frankly," he says.

Told that it seems he has taken more joy in the game of late, as Jellybean once did, Kobe thinks for a moment, then nods. "It's interesting, and you're right—my dad just exuded joy for the game," Kobe says. "But I would say I love the game even more, because I love the game so much I did it every day, nonstop for hours and hours and hours and hours."

It's interesting that he equates joy with hard work, as if it must be earned. In Kobe's world, anything that comes easy is, by its very nature, not worth treasuring. He sees his role on the Lakers in the final third of his career as, in essence, a— in chief. "You can't afford to placate people," he explains, his voice rising. "You can't afford to do that. You're a leader. You're not here to be a social butterfly. You're here to get them to the promised land. A lot of people shy away from that because a lot of people want to be liked by everybody. I want to be liked too. But I know that years from now they'll appreciate how I pushed them to get us to that end result."

Bryant sits back, letting the thoughts sit in the air for a moment. Then he continues. "It's never easy, man. This s— is hard. So when players look in the distance and see us winning championships and see us celebrating and having a good time, they think, Oh, this is what leadership is, this is how you win, everyone gets along, we're all buddy-buddy, we all hang out, blah, blah."

Bryant shifts in his seat, leans forward. "No it's not like that. You talk to Lamar [Odom], Adam Morrison. We were at each other's throats every day. Challenging each other, confronting each other. That's how it gets done. But that's hard, because it's uncomfortable, right? It's uncomfortable."

This approach—Bryant likens it to the unpleasant task of telling a dinner mate he has "s— in his teeth"—does not go over well all the time. Like with Dwight Howard, for example. Others appreciate it. During filming, Chopra interviewed a number of Bryant's teammates, current and former, and he asked them to describe Bryant in three words. After each interview Kobe would text Chopra, eager to hear what people said. Most answered with some variation of "the ultimate competitor" or "killer instinct." But when Chopra asked Steve Nash, he said something different. After thinking for a moment, Nash answered, slowly, in three beats: "Mother... f—... a—."

Kobe thought this was awesome.

It's easy to forget just how much Bryant has changed during his career. He evolved from a brash kid with a baby fro and a killer Michael Jordan impression to a star who won titles with Shaq—even if he was ill-suited to the sidekick role the big man relegated him to. Then came the rape case—ultimately dropped—in Eagle, Colo. All the sponsors fled except Nike, which he'd signed with only a week earlier. Kobe turned inward, became the pure competitor he was destined to be. For roughly the next five years we saw the Mercenary Kobe, and it was glorious. He berated teammates, demeaned opponents, scored 81 points because he could. Finally, in 2009, he won a title on his own terms. The burden lifted. And yet, the image that sticks out from covering that championship is of Bryant, at 2 a.m. during the series, sitting in a hotel lobby with a Corona, among friends but yet still alone, staring off into the distance.

Some people are forced into isolation. Kobe seeks it. He refers to himself as "just a kid from Italy." He speaks with pride of growing up in his backyard, shooting imaginary jumpers, forging his confidence in one-on-none situations. Talk to him now about solitude, and he acknowledges the role it's played in his life. "Being alone, you can't hide, man, you can't fool yourself," he says.

So Kobe found his drive in being different, in being alone. That's why he studies the iconoclasts. It's why he's close to so few people in the NBA. And it's why, while some like Phil Jackson think he will prosper upon leaving the game, others aren't so sure. "You know how it's been hard for Jordan in retirement?" says one GM. "It's going to be way worse to be Kobe. He has fewer friends and the same competitive drive. At least MJ likes to golf and play cards."

Now it's Sunday afternoon, Kobe's fifth full day in Shanghai, and he's burned out. It's been a long week of glad-handing, photo shoots, design summits, late-night dinners, and court christenings. Slowly, Bryant lowers himself onto a couch in the VVIP room, his legs sore from a morning workout. Asked how he processes all this—the adulation, the fans, the statues of him—he looks surprised. Statues? He hadn't noticed them, he claims. It's been too crazy. (Later, on the ride home, he will turn to the crew and ask if they saw the statues. Heads will nod. "What do you think of them?" Bryant will ask. "They're cool," Nico will assure him. "Yeah, they're cool," Bryant will say, then pause. "Right?")

All week Kobe has been trying hard. Playing a role. At one event after another he fixes his face into an awkward perma-grin, as he turns and acknowledges one screaming fan section after another. He raises his hands in twin Vs. During the player talent evaluations, he is dead set on being a positive influence. In keeping with the spirit of Kobe being a Force for Good, he insists on playing the role of a "mentor," rather than a Simon Cowell figure. So when it's time to cut players, Kobe chooses the ones who move on, rather than singling out those who won't. His commentary as he watches the kids bungle layups and go one-on-four is forcedly diplomatic. "It's going on right now." … "Oooh, had a good look."

He can only contain himself for so long, though. Which brings us back to the one-on-one game against the Chinese teen, back on Wednesday night, four nights earlier, the one that went viral. The title of the video when it showed up on sports blogs was along the lines of "Kobe destroys Chinese fans at one-on-one!" It showed Bryant draining deep threes against a lanky kid, and it all fit in perfectly with the Kobe narrative. The Mamba Mythology.

Only that's not what happened. What actually transpired was that Bryant became increasingly geeked as the night went on, watching all these kids chuck up jumpers. First he began dribbling a ball between his legs. Then he bit his lip. Then, when the show was supposed to be wrapping up, he grabbed the mike from the emcee. "They probably haven't seen me play in a while, so we'll do a little one-on-one game," Kobe said, and this was true because no one had seen him play competitively in nearly a year. Not Gotham. Not his handlers. "We used to call the game 'sunrise' in Philly," Bryant continued. "Whoever scores stays on."

The two emcees were surprised but went with it as Kobe extricated himself from his headset and took some practice shots. Then Bryant handpicked the three best opponents among the 30 campers, and they began a rotating game of one-on-one, winner stays on, to five buckets. The crowd, as you can imagine, went bonkers. At first Kobe looked rusty. Really rusty. His jumpers hit the front iron. He threw up an airball. He ended up backing down the kids and shooting five-foot jump hooks. It looked as if maybe his comeback was not as far along as advertised. Then, slowly, Bryant came alive. He sank deep into a stance on D, he chased down long rebounds, pivoted, and fired up high-arcing baseline fadeaways. Against a particularly frenetic guard, he backed him down, then dribbled around the kid's back and spun to score, sending the crowd and emcees into spasms of joy. This is what they came to see. As Kobe will explain later, "They want to know what it's like to actually see it, up close. To have that experience."

There was only one problem with the narrative: Kobe lost. This is the part you don't see on the viral videos. He thought he had the game in hand, with four points tallied in a game to five. Then the tallest of the Chinese kids, wearing a number 10 jersey, sank an impressive 17-foot fadeaway bank shot on Kobe to score his third point. After which number 10 proceeded to score on the other two kids while Kobe watched helplessly from the sideline. Ball game. Some random Chinese kid just beat Kobe in a one-on-one contest.

Clearly, this could not stand. While the kid raised his arms in celebration, Kobe gave him exactly three courtesy claps before grabbing the mike again. He was no longer smiling, no longer jovial. "O.K., we're going to play again," Kobe announced. "First to five and we'll play like I did growing up. Full court." The two emcees looked both surprised and concerned. "Are you sure?" one asked. On the sideline Team Kobe stood up. Full court on a reconstructed knee? When Kobe hadn't played competitively in almost a year? You could just see the headlines: Kobe reinjures knee while taping bizarre Chinese game show.

There was no dissuading Kobe, though. Similarly, there was no discussion about the other two kids from the previous game. They were shooed off the court. This was personal. So the campers cleared the floor for a showdown between one of the five greatest players in NBA history and a kid from Who-Knows-Where, China. Again Kobe started slow, missing his shot for outs, but it was clear that there was no way he was losing this time. At one point he blocked the kid's shot out-of-bounds and, without pausing—and without regard for the rules—took possession himself. Then it happened. He nailed a 23-footer. Running back down the court, he started moving his shoulders. Feeling it. Then a 22-footer. Now Kobe was firing the finger guns and licking his fingertips. A 26-footer followed and the place erupted. Then a 30-footer. Sure the lanky kid answered with a layup, and answered again with a three, but Kobe wasn't really guarding him, and it didn't matter anyway. We all knew what was coming. And so on game point, Bryant pivoted and pivoted again just above the free throw line and then faded that Kobe fade and unleashed that gooseneck follow-through and the ball splashed in and the crowd went berserk and the watching players pumped their fists while Kobe stood, arms outstretched as if he'd just won his sixth ring and not an informal game of one-on-one in Shanghai. Afterward, in true Kobe fashion, he took the mike and explained to the kid that he needed to work on his left hand, making sure the emcees translated it correctly.

It made for great theater. All week Kobe tried to be supportive, to be the good cop. But only on this night did he truly communicate, giving them what they came for, something they could actually learn from. He could have showed up, done the grip-and-grin, and headed back to the hotel. Instead he went nearly an hour over the allotted taping time and ended up at midcourt, arms around four different players, in a sweat-soaked shirt and—since he'd given away his shoes—floppy white socks.

Here was the truth behind the Mamba Mythology. The message behind the message. That in reality it's never easy. That sometimes you gotta challenge some punk teenager to a double-or-nothing game. And then you have to elbow him in the post, and cheat on the out-of-bounds play, and impose your will on the poor sap, because when it comes down to it, sometimes that's what it takes to win, son.

打出
名堂
RISE

Bryant's competitive drive was always on display, even at a 2014 promotional event in China.

After scoring 60 points against Utah in his last NBA game, Bryant said goodbye to the Lakers fans at Staples Center. At 37 years and 234 days old, he became the oldest player ever to score 60 or more points in a game.

LOS ANGELES LAKERS
SuperDrink
24

vs
00 PM
PT
BRYANT
8

Bryant poses with his family at halftime after both his number 24 and number 8 jerseys were retired at Staples Center in 2017.

caption?

Shaquille O'Neal, Bryant, and Phil Jackson during a ceremony to unveil O'Neal's statue at Staples Center in 2017.

Excerpted from Sports Illustrated, July 16, 2018

Fantastic Voyage

No longer draining daggers for the Lakers, Kobe Bryant—the self-styled Black Mamba—is now an entertainment mogul with a friendlier mission: transporting kids to magical worlds

BY LEE JENKINS

The man who fashioned himself a killer snake wants to raise your children.

Like most grand ambitions in 2018, it all starts with a podcast. But since the podcast belongs to Kobe Bean Bryant, it is a bigger production than the common download. Seven actors, two keyboard players, and an Emmy-nominated writer sit around a conference table with bagels and LaCroix.

They are on the second floor of a beige office building in Costa Mesa, Calif., but the space feels more like an Arts District loft: exposed pipes, Persian rugs, Manzanita trees, twinkle lights. Black-and-white photographs of J.K. Rowling and Walt Disney, Michael Jackson and Oprah Winfrey, line the entryway. A story room, with writers lounging on gray sofas and scribbling across grease boards, is hidden behind thick curtains. A sign that reads "ZEN AS F—" leans against the wall in the production studio, waiting to go up.

One building over is the headquarters of the Chargers, arguably the most irrelevant institution in Southland sports, neighbors with perhaps the most popular. Between these bizarre bedfellows is a coffee shop called The Lost Bean. Bryant works at a black desk in a glass cube, scrawling notes on a legal pad because he doesn't like to type. He is preparing for a table read of *The Punies*, an ensemble podcast for children that he conceived two years ago while watching *A Charlie Brown Thanksgiving* with his family, an annual tradition. He began jotting descriptions of characters for his athletically inclined Peanuts: Puny Pete, the lovable loser; B.B. LaBelle, the bossy leader; Gordo Lockett, the affable oddball; Kimberly Spice, the smart one; Lilly Sparks, the hyper one; Clark Mayhoff, the troublesome one. The crew has nothing

Kobe Bryant made history in 2018 by becoming the first professional athlete to win an Academy Award. He collaborated with Glen Keane on the animated short film *Dear Basketball*, based on the poem announcing the Laker's retirement.

to invest the time and really work on it. That's why we don't do many things here. But the things we do, we turn over and over and over again." When puppeteers originally introduced him to his "Musecage" co-star, a high-pitched purple snake named Little Mamba, Bryant didn't approve of the character's texture and requested that its fabric be changed.

"The first time he came over here, I thought for sure he'd be disappointed, because he'd been visiting bigger studios and our place is just a tiny duplex in West Hollywood," says Glen Keane, the famed animator behind *The Little Mermaid*, *Beauty and the Beast*, *Aladdin*, and *Pocahontas*. "He stopped in our little living room, transformed into a story room, and I imagined him thinking, What am I getting myself into? This doesn't look like a big-time studio. He said, 'It's perfect. It's real.'"

Bryant hired Keane to animate *Dear Basketball*, a love poem that required two drafts. In the first, Bryant was angry at the game for abandoning him. In the final version, he was grateful to it, for sticking with him so long. When they won the Academy Award, Keane glanced at Bryant, frozen in his tux. "I'd never seen him the way he was in that moment," Keane recalls. "Usually, he's very connected and engaged, but he wasn't moving. I told him, 'Kobe, we've got to go, they only give us 45 seconds.'" The mention of time broke his daze. After staggering to the stage, Bryant located the clock, which seemed to steady him. Keane noticed him staring at the numbers, visibly counting down. He was trying to beat another buzzer.

"What should I do next?" Bryant asked Keane after the Oscars.

"We did a short," Keane replied. "Go long."

The Granity novels will feature gods, kings, wizards, and a whole lot of regular nine-to-12-year-old kids, but Kobe Bryant is missing. "He's not in any of this," says chief marketing officer Molly Carter. "The way he processes emotion and dealt with obstacles, that's what shows up." There is also no Mamba character in *The Punies*, though when Keane read the script, he still saw Bryant all over the page.

"It's a little like Dorothy with the Tin Man, the Scarecrow, and the Cowardly Lion," Keane says. "There are aspects of her in all those characters, and there are aspects of him in all these characters, even if he doesn't know it. They're like an exploded Kobe. They've all got a little piece of him." You can sense his vulnerability in Puny Pete, which he often disguised, and his conviction through B.B. LaBelle, which he never did. In "Coaches Are People Too," a duet sung by Kimberly and Clark, Kobe seems less like the guy Mike D'Antoni knew, and more like the one Gianna does:

> They may yell and scream, they may blow their whistle.
> They may throw their clipboard like a ballistic missile.
> But coaching is hard, that's a matter of fact.
> Takes time, takes patience, it's like herding cats.

After the 70-minute table read, the actors stare anxiously at Bryant, who finally opens his eyes. "That was awesome," he says. "You played off each other really well. You were really smooth. Take the material home, study it, and you'll fall more in line with your characters. You'll get comfortable and find some beats where you can add a little laughter. More work to be done, but we'll get there." As they scatter, he approaches them individually. "Work on your lines together, two hours a day. Practice." He wonders whether, in the surfboard sketch, they should record their parts while standing on actual boards.

When they leave, Bryant retreats to his glass cube. He has to make a scheduled call. Back behind his desk, he punches in the number and waits, until Steven Spielberg answers.

Despite many who believed he would have trouble transitioning to life beyond the court, Bryant seemed content with life after basketball.

THE PASSING OF AN ICON

Bryant and daughter Gianna at a Lakers-Hawks game in 2019.

Chapter 5

Excerpted from SI.com, January 26, 2020

The Mamba Generation

No performer had a bigger impact on today's NBA players than Kobe Bryant, whose game was widely emulated and whose recognition meant everything

BY CHRIS MANNIX

He had been retired for two years, and yet as Boston battled Cleveland in the 2018 Eastern Conference finals, members of the Celtics' organization were grumbling about Kobe Bryant. Between Games 2 and 3, Bryant had released a new episode of *Detail*, the ESPN+ show he helmed that did deep dives on young NBA stars.

The subject was Jayson Tatum, Boston's rising rookie. Bryant's breakdown focused on Game 2. Tatum admitted to watching it dozens of times, so many, Celtics coaches noted, that for the remainder of the series he appeared to be incorporating Bryant's notes into his game.

Kobe, team officials muttered, somewhat tongue in cheek, couldn't have waited until after the season?

Bryant was killed in a helicopter crash in Calabasas, Calif., on Sunday. He was 41. The aircraft went down in a remote field off of Las Virgenes around 10 a.m. Bryant's daughter, 13-year-old Gianna, was among those who died in the crash.

There are no words for such an unspeakable tragedy.

Not since Roberto Clemente has a sports luminary passed so tragically.

You mourn Bryant, a father of four. The transition from elite athlete to whatever comes next can be difficult. Bryant made it look easy. He founded Granity Studios, a multimedia company. He won an Oscar. He won an Emmy. He opened a sports academy. Then another. He opened a publishing house. He became the world's most famous AAU coach.

You are overwhelmed with grief for Gianna, GiGi to Bryant, for a life taken too soon. In interviews, Bryant has said he is often asked

Bryant's retired jerseys, hanging from the rafters at Staples Center, took on added significance following the star's death. (Inset) Michael Jordan speaks at a memorial service held on February 24, 2020, in honor of Bryant, his daughter Gianna, and the seven others who died in a helicopter crash.

about not having a son, a male heir to continue his legacy. When he is, he will point to GiGi, his basketball-obsessed daughter. Recently, a video circulated of Bryant sitting next to GiGi at a Lakers game, just a father and daughter talking shop.

You hurt for his wife, Vanessa, and the three daughters Bryant leaves behind.

These are the people closest to Bryant, yet they represent a fraction of the people he has touched. Bryant leaves behind a complicated legacy, but for young athletes could not have been simpler. A generation lost a hero on Sunday, thousands of basketball players who grew up spinning along baselines and firing up picture-perfect midrange jump shots lost the legend that showed them how. "My generation, it was Dr. J," Wizards coach Scott Brooks said. "And then maybe Michael Jordan was a little bit after. The generation now is Kobe. He's exactly what everybody dreamed about playing [against] on the playground."

Thousands of people gathered to pay respects to all of the lives lost, leaving balloons, flowers, and other tributes outside Staples Center.

James Harden used to rush home to watch Bryant's games. Tatum called Bryant the reason he played. Stephen Curry has sought Bryant's advice on how to manage injuries. Draymond Green went to him to ask for help keeping his emotions in check. Just last month, Spencer Dinwiddie nearly went bonkers when he saw Bryant sitting courtside in Brooklyn. On Sunday, an emotional Doc Rivers, his voice cracking, noted the hurt in the eyes of his youngest players. Said Rivers, "That just tells you how far his reach was."

In Los Angeles, the Lakers' plane touched down, news of Bryant's passing breaking on the six-hour flight from Philadelphia. LeBron James emerged, in tears. He dabbed his eyes with tissue paper. He hugged Kurt Rambis on the tarmac. Not a full day had passed since James jumped Bryant on the NBA's all-time scoring list. Bryant's last tweet was to congratulate James on the accomplishment. In many ways, Bryant was James' peer. Bryant, James said on Saturday night, "will always be the guy I looked up to when I was in grade school."

"Seeing him come straight out of high school, he is someone that I used as inspiration," James said. "It was like, 'wow.' Seeing a kid, 17 years old, come into the NBA and trying to make an impact on a franchise, I used it as motivation. He helped me before he even knew of me because of what he was able to do. So, just to be able to, at this point of my career, to share the same jersey that he wore, be with this historical franchise and just represent the purple and gold, it's very humbling and it's dope."

Tributes to Bryant have poured in from everywhere. Barack Obama offered his condolences. Chants of Kobe reverberated at the Pro Bowl. A half a world away, soccer star Neymar flashed a 2-4 after a goal, a nod to Bryant's jersey number. The NBA elected to play its games Sunday, but each game opened the same. A 24-second violation for one team. An eight-second backcourt violation for the other.

All to honor No. 24.

And No. 8.

The NBA will pay its respects to Bryant at the All-Star Game next month, and there is an easy way how. Bryant wore two numbers during his 20-year NBA career. The All-Star Game has two teams. LeBron James' team can wear No. 24. Giannis Antetokounmpo's can wear No. 8. There will be 24 players in Chicago who grew up worshiping Bryant. A fitting tribute would be to let all of them wear his number.

Vanessa Bryant speaks at the memorial service held at Staples Center.

A billboard outside Staples Center on January 28, 2020.

Mamba Forever
RIGHT LANE
BUSES
RIGHT TURNS
ONLY

Excerpted from SI.com, January 26, 2020

Remembering Kobe and Gianna

Los Angeles Lakers legend Kobe Bryant and his 13-year-old daughter, Gianna, were tragically killed in a helicopter crash. Michael Rosenberg reflects on the loss for Bryant's family, the NBA, and the world

BY MICHAEL ROSENBERG

Thirteen-year-old Gianna Bryant and her father are gone, and that is not quite how the Bryants' story will be told, but it's how we should think about it first. We all get one life, none more important than any other. Gianna did not have the chance to live hers, and the sadness is unbearable.

For her mom, Vanessa, and for her sisters Natalia, Bianka, and Capri, there will be a million tributes, and all will be insufficient. What do you say? What does it matter?

Their thoughts are theirs, to form over time, and to share only if they ever feel the desire. Our thoughts about the Bryant family should start with Gianna, and nobody understood that better than Kobe Bryant.

From a distance, especially when he was young, Kobe was easy to caricature as the kind of man who would only be happy raising a boy, and then, only a boy like him. He was legendarily competitive, the most committed athlete in his sport, a proud and self-described "alpha male" who had an uneven relationship with his own father. But one reason Kobe Bryant was so alluring was that he didn't just do what society expected him to do. He coached girls' basketball and became perhaps the sport's most prominent fan. He told Jimmy Kimmel that when strangers said he needed a son to carry his legacy, he had a quick answer: Gianna could handle it herself.

One of the hardest tasks for any of us is figuring out who we are. Kobe went beyond that: he always seemed to know who he would

Bryant and Gianna watch a game between the Nets and Hawks on December 21, 2019, at Barclays Center.

Michael Jordan stands nearby as Vanessa Bryant speaks on behalf of her late husband at the 2021 Basketball Hall of Fame induction ceremony. Kobe Bryant was posthumously inducted, along with fellow stars Tim Duncan and Kevin Garnett, among others.

become. He knew it when he turned pro out of Lower Merion High School, back when nobody did that; the best basketball prospect in the world at that time, Tim Duncan, decided to return to Wake Forest for his senior season. A *SportsCenter* anchor quoted an anonymous scout saying the kid had made a mistake. Well.

You could say there were better players, but that was missing the point. Kobe was not about efficiency or advanced metrics or even those best-ever debates. His career was about bending the game to his will. He won three titles with Shaq and two more without. In the middle, of course, he was accused of sexually assaulting a woman in Colorado; charges were dropped, and he settled a civil suit. That is part of Bryant's story, but analyzing the particulars of it today feels both reductive and insensitive to everybody.

He thought he was the best player on the Lakers before he joined the starting lineup. He knew he wanted to marry a teenager named Vanessa Laine when so many said it was a mistake. He set his goal to be the best player ever before he was close to being the best player in the NBA. He saw the Lakers as his team even when teammate Shaquille O'Neal was the most dominant player of his era. He envisioned a happy, creative, post-playing life before he stopped playing.

The basketball court is where he found solace and developed an unwavering belief in himself. The easy comparison, stylistically, was always Michael Jordan; Bryant copied MJ without apology and with stunning success. But the best comparisons were mental, and they transcended sports: Jordan, Tiger Woods, those athletes who expected success, no matter what was happening, because expecting to succeed was their core belief.

We will remember Kobe in a series of indelible moments: not flinching when Matt Barnes faked inbounding the ball into his face; shooting free throws with a torn Achilles; scoring 60 points in his final game. He had two numbers retired. For a generation, the Lakers will always be his team.

The NBA's Banana Boat generation that came after him—LeBron James, Dwyane Wade, Chris Paul, Carmelo Anthony—is a brotherhood, and that is admirable. But damn, there was nothing quite like the feeling in an arena when Kobe Bryant had the ball in his hands with the clock winding down. They have a word in L.A. for the other nine guys on the court at that moment. Extras.

What a life, but more, what a way to live life. This is what we'll miss, and this, at its core, is why the grief over Bryant's death is so profound. This guy had it figured out. He knew how you were supposed to feel when you woke up in the morning. He understood the value of a day. He could make anybody in his orbit understand, too.

Imagine having that man as your dad.

Heartbreaking is the word we use most often when describing the death of a child, and it never feels close to adequate. We will never know the woman that Gianna Bryant would have become. We know her father would have urged her to become whatever she wanted, to dream as big as she could, and then dream bigger than that.

KOBE
BRYANT
LOS ANGELES LAKERS
CLASS OF 2020

Grammy Award winner Ne-Yo performs as Kobe Bryant is honored during the Basketball Hall of Fame induction ceremony.

April 27, 1998

May 29, 2000

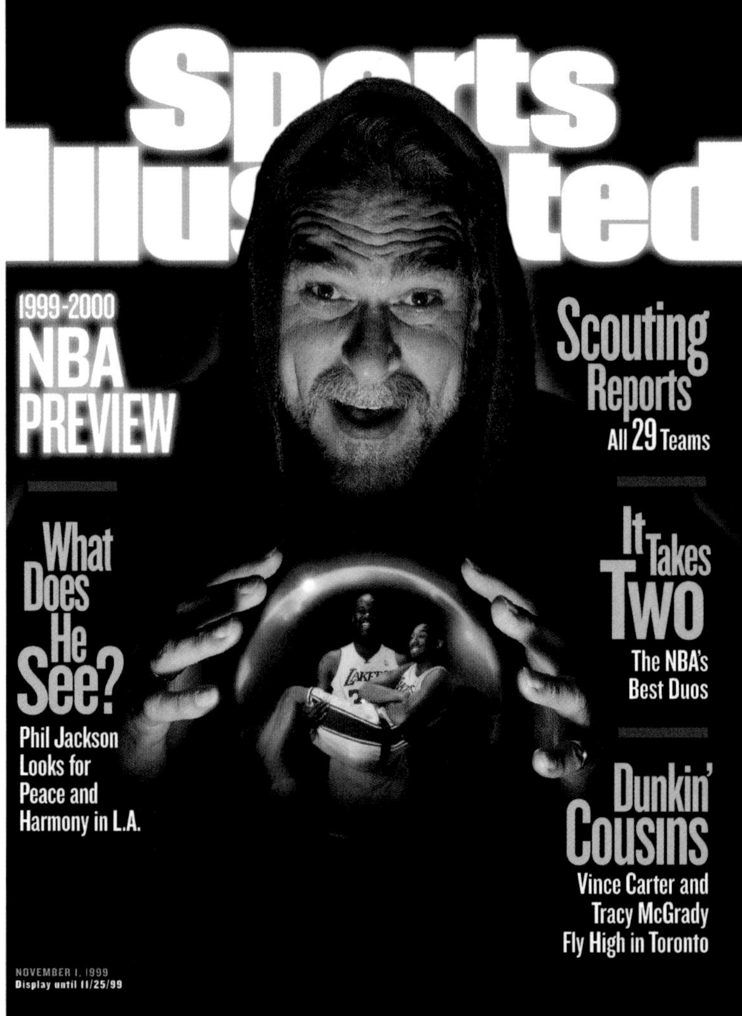

November 1, 1999

June 12, 2000

June 25, 2001

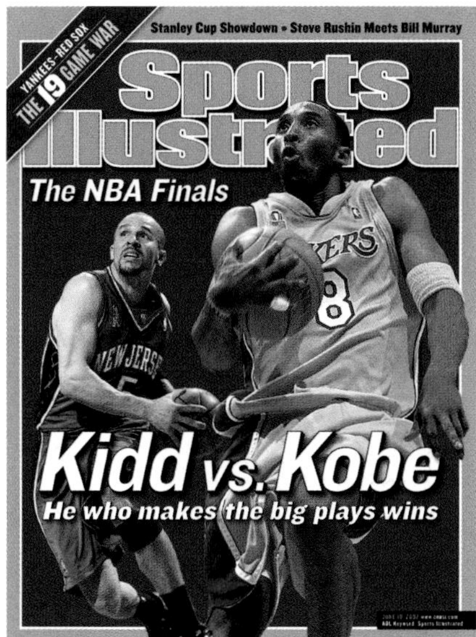

June 10, 2002

March 3, 2003

July 28, 2003

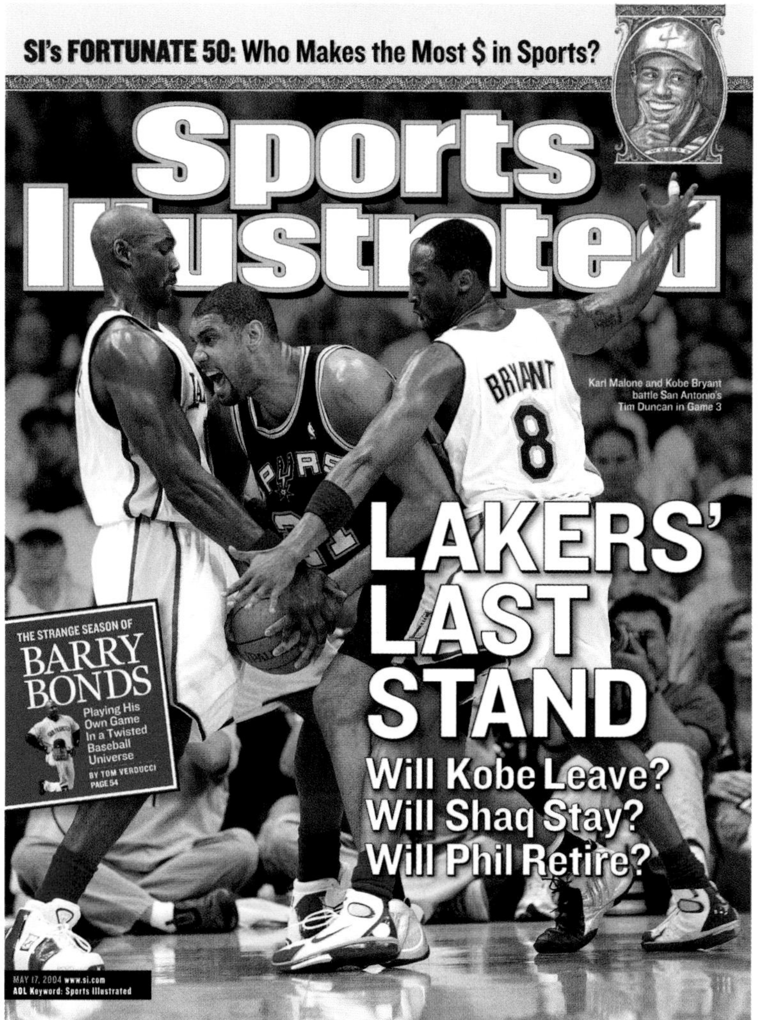

May 17, 2004

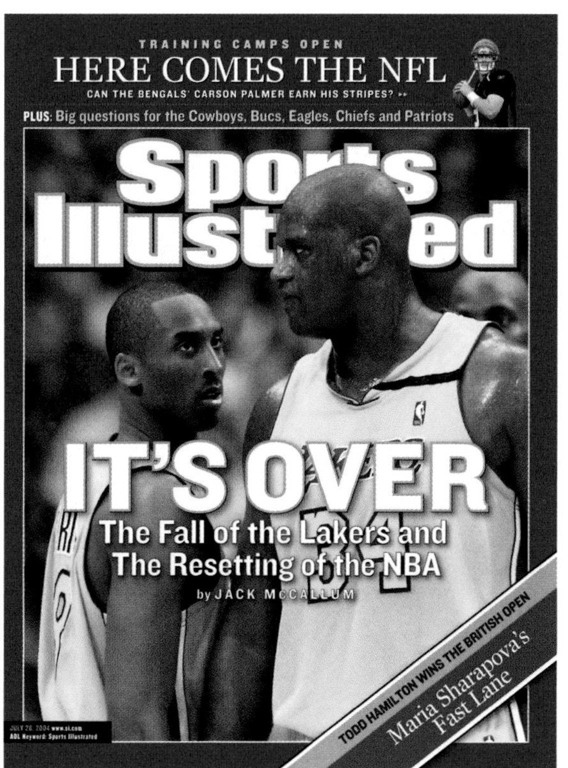

July 26, 2004

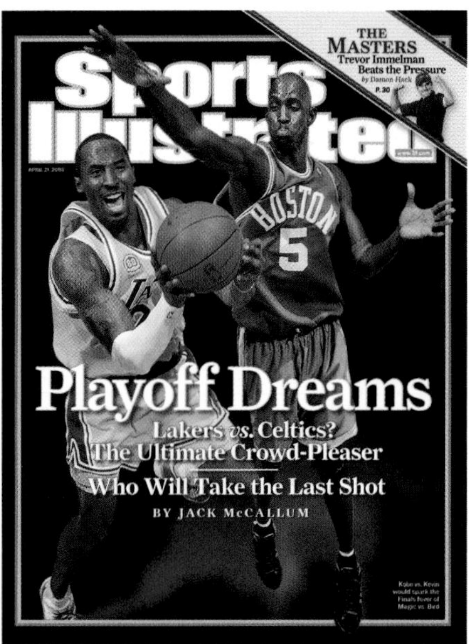

April 21, 2008

October 27, 2008

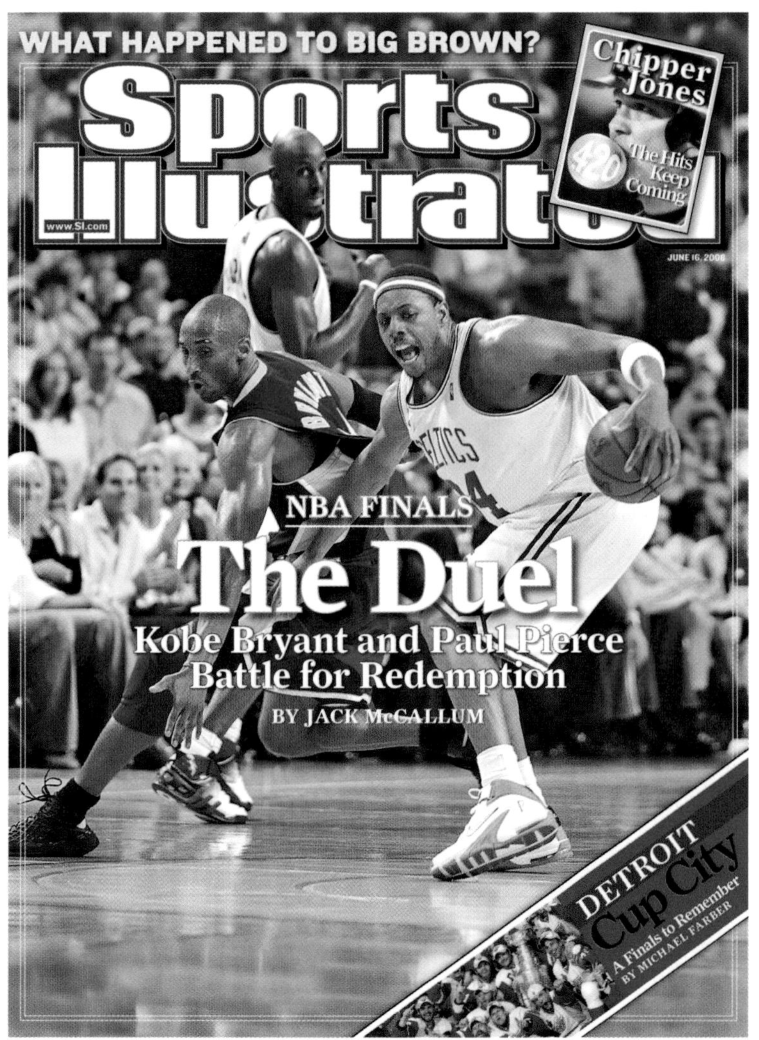

June 16, 2008

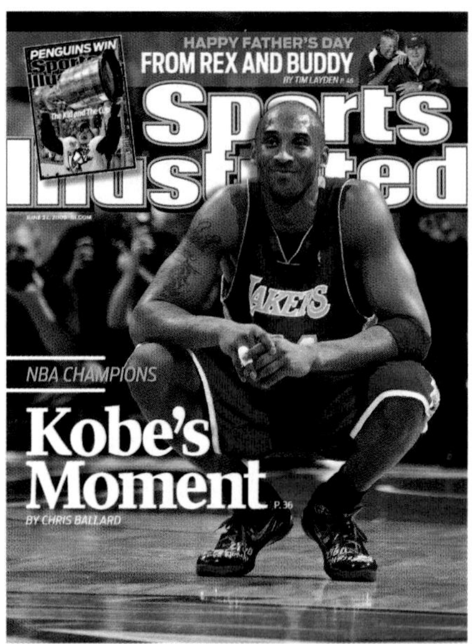

June 22, 2009

June 28, 2010

February 21, 2011

October 26, 2015

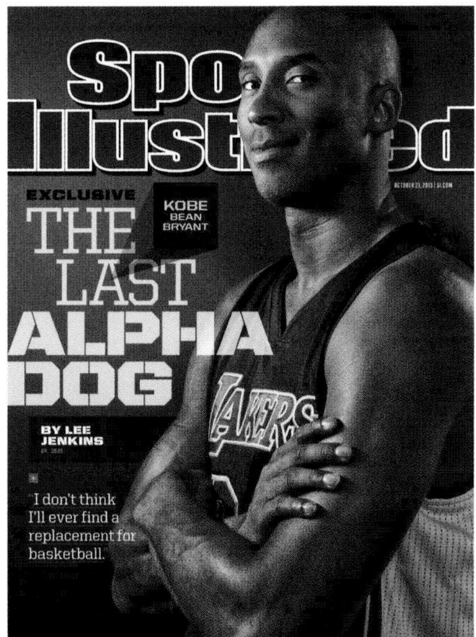

October 21, 2013

August 25, 2014

Photo Credits

Bill Frakes: Pages 170-71; Bob Rosato: Pages 77, 104, 138-39, 140-41, 148, 150-51, 155, 158, 162-63, 183; David E. Klutho: Pages 46-47; John Biever: Pages 60, 63, 68, 100, 102-03, 126-27, 168-69; John W. McDonough: Pages 1, 6-7, 30-32, 34, 69, 80-81, 84, 96-97, 105-109, 115, 119, 129-31, 133, 142-43, 152-53, 166-67, 174, 184-87, 202-03, 217-21; Manny Millan: Pages 9, 18-19, 35, 39, 62; Peter Read Miller: Pages 113, 123, 160-61, 164-65; Robert Beck: Pages 4-5, 50-51, 85-87, 94-95, 110-11, 116-17, 213; Walter Iooss Jr.: Pages 2, 21, 34, 36-37, 44-45, 52-55, 64-67, 72-73, 232.

Additional photography: Allen Berezovsky/Getty Images: Pages 214-15; AFP via Getty Images: Pages 48-49; Ed Andriesk/Getty Images: Pages 92-93; Fred Lee/Getty Images: Pages 200-01; Hector Mata/AFP via Getty Images: Pages 14-15; J. Emilio Flores/Getty Images: Page 89; Jeff Gross/Getty Images: Page 177; Jeff Haynes/AFP via Getty Images: Pages 13, 70-71; Kevork Djansezian/Getty Images: Pages 206-07; Lisa Blumenfeld/Getty Images: Page 78; Maddie Meyer/Getty Images: Pages 224, 226-27; Matt Campbell/AFP via Getty Images: Page 12; Maxx Wolfson/Getty Images: Pages 204-05; Mike Nelson/AFP via Getty Images: Page 24; Paul Bereswill/Getty Images: Page 223; Robyn Beck/AFP via Getty Images: Page 91; Steve Granitz/WireImage: Page 209; Steve Grayson/WireImage: Page 10; Vincent Laforet/AFP via Getty Images: Pages 16-17.

Library of Congress Cataloging-in-Publication Data available upon request.

This book is available in quantity at special discounts for your group or organization. For further information, contact:

Triumph Books LLC
814 North Franklin Street
Chicago, Illinois 60610
(312) 337-0747
www.triumphbooks.com

Printed in U.S.A.
ISBN: 978-1-62937-949-4

Kobe Bean Bryant,
1978–2020

Sports Illustrated™